Essential SQA Exam Practice

National 5 Modern Studies

Practice Questions & Exam Papers

Questions & Papers

Practise **25+ extended questions** covering every question type

Complete **2 practice papers** that mirror the real SQA exams

Frank Cooney
Kenneth Hannah

HODDER GIBSON
AN HACHETTE UK COMPANY

The Publishers would like to thank the following for permission to reproduce copyright material.

Photo credits: p.7(l) © iodrakon - stock.adobe.com; p.7(r) © szefei – 123rf; p.13(l) © Monkey Business via Thinkstock/Getty Images; p13(r) © Cathy Yeulet – 123rf; p.40 (l) © kurhan – 123rf; p.40(r) © Rob – stock.adobe.com.

Acknowledgements

Every effort has been made to trace all copyright holders, but if any have been inadvertently overlooked, the Publishers will be pleased to make the necessary arrangements at the first opportunity.

Although every effort has been made to ensure that website addresses are correct at time of going to press, Hodder Gibson cannot be held responsible for the content of any website mentioned in this book. It is sometimes possible to find a relocated web page by typing in the address of the home page for a website in the URL window of your browser.

Hachette UK's policy is to use papers that are natural, renewable and recyclable products and made from wood grown in well-managed forests and other controlled sources. The logging and manufacturing processes are expected to conform to the environmental regulations of the country of origin.

Orders: please contact Bookpoint Ltd, 130 Park Drive, Milton Park, Abingdon, Oxon OX14 4SE. Telephone: (44) 01235 827827. Fax: (44) 01235 400401. Email education@bookpoint.co.uk. Lines are open from 9 a.m. to 5 p.m., Monday to Friday, with a 24-hour message answering service. Visit our website at www.hoddereducation.co.uk. If you have queries or questions that aren't about an order you can contact us at hoddergibson@hodder.co.uk

© Frank Cooney and Kenneth Hannah 2019

First published in 2019 by

Hodder Gibson, an imprint of Hodder Education

An Hachette UK Company

211 St Vincent Street

Glasgow, G2 5QY

Impression number	5	4	3	2	1
Year	2023	2022	2021	2020	2019

Illustrations by Aptara Inc.

Typeset in India by Aptara Inc.

Printed and bound by CPI Group (UK) Ltd, Croydon CR0 4YY

A catalogue record for this title is available from the British Library.

ISBN: 978 1 5104 7190 0

We are an approved supplier on the Scotland Excel framework.

Schools can find us on their procurement system as:

Hodder & Stoughton Limited t/a Hodder Gibson.

CONTENTS

National 5 Modern Studies

Welcome to your revision of National 5 Modern Studies.

Working your way through this Exam Practice book should help you to maximise your marks in the knowledge and understanding and evaluating sources sections of your SQA exam.

Section 1 will provide general advice on what is required for the five styles of questions you will answer (describe, explain, support and oppose views, provide support for valid conclusions, and give justification for decisions). This will include exemplar student answers with relevant advice on what you need to do to improve your grades, followed by a range of exam questions with marked examples on pages 3–21.

Section 2 includes two full exam papers with marking instructions for you to practise on. You may wish to time yourself to make sure that you can answer questions in the time allotted. This will improve your time management and help you avoid having to rush your questions, or even worse, miss out some questions.

A summary of the exam course follows but, first, here are some common-sense tips to prepare you for the exam.

Study skills – what you need to know to pass exams

When you study and revise, do you use the time wisely and productively, or do you find you cannot concentrate and look for excuses to do something else instead?

Start your revision in good time and do not leave it to the last moment. Make a revision timetable that sets out a balanced **plan** of study and 'you time'.

So, good – you have started early! This gives you time to organise the **first stage** of revision. You should use the following: an up-to-date textbook, class notes/handouts and slide shows. Find a copy of the course outlines of the topics your exam will cover – you should make sure that there are no gaps in your knowledge and skills.

Make sure you know what to expect in the exam by being able to answer the following:

▶ What type of questions will be asked, and how much time should you devote to each question?

▶ Which topics are your strongest and which are your weakest?

How the exam paper is structured

You are now ready to begin the **second stage**. You should make short summary notes from your textbook or course materials for each of your three topics. You may type them out or write them using different-coloured pens. Remember to use mind-maps etc., as these are excellent memory aids. This will be time-consuming, but will be worth it as these will be the only notes you will use for your future knowledge revision. You should also practise skills-based questions from previous exam papers.

You are now ready for the **third stage**, which will take place close to your exam. Research has shown that we feel more positive and retain information better if we are active. Music stimulates the brain and provides a good feeling. So you could begin each revision session by walking or dancing around your room, listening to your favourite songs. **Try it, it works!** Sitting gazing at notes will lead to daydreaming – your mind will wander and you will find it hard to focus.

'The thing that matters most must never be at the mercy of the things that matter the least.'

JW von Goethe (nineteenth-century German writer)

Personal checklist/action plan

▶ Get your materials ready.

▶ Always know what you are trying to learn.

▶ Get rid of distractions.

▶ Maintain focus.

▶ Think about it.

▶ Revise from the beginning.

▶ Take notes.

▶ Use this book to Practise, Practise, Practise!

Your National 5 Modern Studies award is an externally marked assessment. It consists of two parts:

National 5 question paper: 80 marks

National 5 assignment: 20 marks

The marks you achieve in the question paper and assignment are added together and an overall mark will indicate a pass or fail. From this, your course award will then be graded.

The exam

The exam paper is split into three sections:

▶ Democracy in Scotland and the United Kingdom

▶ Social Issues in the United Kingdom

▶ International Issues.

You will usually have studied one topic from each of the three sections above, and the knowledge and understanding questions will be on the topics shown in the table below.

Section	Choice one	Choice two
1 Democracy in Scotland and the United Kingdom	A Democracy in Scotland	B Democracy in the United Kingdom
2 Social Issues in the United Kingdom	C Social Inequality	D Crime and the Law
3 International Issues	E World Powers	F World Issues
Total marks available:	80 marks	

To gain the course award, you must pass all units and course assessments.

The question paper

You will have 2 hours and 20 minutes to complete the question paper, with a total of 80 marks allocated. There are 30 marks available for evaluation of sources questions and 50 for knowledge and understanding questions. One section, for example Democracy in Scotland, may have 28 knowledge marks and the other two sections 26 knowledge marks each.

As stated, the paper will be divided into three sections. For each section, you will answer three knowledge and understanding questions and one evaluation of sources question. The three knowledge and understanding questions will be as follows:

▶ **Describe** (worth either 4 or 6 marks)
For example:

Describe, **in detail**, **two** ways in which the police try to reduce crime levels.　6 marks

▶ **Explain** (worth either 6 or 8 marks)
For example:

Explain, **in detail**, why many people in the UK live in poverty.

You should give a **maximum** of **three** reasons in your answer.　8 marks

▶ **Evaluation of sources** (worth 10 marks each)
The three styles of questions are:

● Using a range of sources of information to support and oppose views, for example:

'The 2015 General Election was a massive disappointment for the Labour Party.' David Trotter

– Give evidence to support David Trotter's view.

– Give evidence from the sources opposed to David Trotter's view.

● Using a range of sources of information to give detailed justifications for decisions, for example:

Which option would you choose?

Give reasons to support your choice and explain why you did not choose the other option.

● Using a range of sources of information to give detailed support for valid conclusions, for example:

You should reach a conclusion about the Electoral College results of 2016 compared to 2012.

Good luck!

KEY AREA INDEX GRID

Content	Practice Questions	Practice Paper 1	Practice Paper 2
Democracy in Scotland and the UK			
Power and decision making	Exemplar	1, 4	
Participation		2, 3, 5, 6	1, 2, 4, 5
Representation	1, 2, 14, 15		
Influence	13		
Voting systems	3, 4		3, 6
Social Inequality			
Nature of social inequality			8
Causes of social inequality	6, 16, 17	10a, 10b	
Consequences of social inequality		8	9
Responses to social inequality	5	9	10
Crime and the Law			
Nature of crime			11
Causes of crime	18	13b	13
Consequences of crime	Exemplar		12
Criminal justice system	7	11	
Responses to crime	13a	12, 13a	
World Powers			
Political system	20	15	16, 17b
Influence of other countries	9	16	17a
Social and economic issues	10	17	15
Effectiveness in tackling social and economic issues	21		
World Issues			
Nature and cause of conflict/issue	11, 22	19	20b
Consequences of conflict/issue	12	18	18, 19
Attempts to resolve conflict/issue			20a
Evaluation of international organisations in tackling conflict/issue	23	20	

Practice makes permanent

In the first part of this section you will receive advice on how to unlock the marks for the knowledge and understanding questions ('describe' and 'explain') and the evaluation of sources questions.

For each style of question, you will be given an example, followed by the opportunity to answer a range of questions.

In your SQA exam you will answer five 'describe', four 'explain' and three evaluation of sources questions. More marks are awarded for knowledge and understanding than evaluation of sources questions, so it is crucial that you have a sound grasp of the content.

The knowledge and understanding questions

Tips for success	Things to avoid
Be aware of the different requirements of 'describe' and 'explain' questions.	Don't confuse the different question types by, for example, giving a 'describe' answer to an 'explain' question.
Only answer the exact question that is set.	Don't turn the question into something it isn't – you won't receive any marks for details or examples that are not relevant.
Develop the points you make with detail.	Don't just write a list of facts – you can only gain a maximum of 2 marks.
Use recent examples to illustrate your knowledge and understanding.	Dated examples should be avoided.
Use the number of marks allocated to each question as a guide to how much you should write.	Don't write too much for the 4 marks answer – you may run out of time on the questions worth the most marks.

Top Tip!

One very developed 'describe' answer can gain 3 marks, and one very developed 'explain' answer can gain 4 marks.

'Describe' questions

>> HOW TO ANSWER

These are the more straightforward type of knowledge and understanding question, and are worth between 4 and 6 marks. All that is required is that you provide the detailed factual knowledge relevant to the question. All 'describe' questions must cover two descriptions.

For a 4- and 6-mark answer, you can be awarded up to 3 marks for a description that is relevant and has exemplification. Two descriptions are necessary for full marks.

Look at the 'describe' question below and see what you need to do to get full marks.

The Scottish Parliament has a range of devolved powers.

Describe, **in detail**, **two** devolved powers of the Scottish Parliament.   6 marks

OR

The UK Parliament has a range of reserved powers.

Describe, **in detail**, **two** reserved powers of the UK Parliament.   6 marks

Top Tip!

As stated, you need to be aware of the new powers given to the Scottish Parliament by the UK Parliament, such as income tax and a range of Social Security payments such as pension credits.

You need to have sound knowledge of the respective powers of the two parliaments, and be aware of the most recent welfare powers granted to the Scottish Parliament. A useful tip is to choose two of the more important powers for your answer.

Below is a list of some of the main devolved and reserved powers:

Devolved	**Reserved**	**Shared**
Education	Defence	Social Security benefits
Health	Immigration	
Law and order	Terrorism	

›› HOW TO ANSWER

ANSWER 1: Scottish Parliament

The Scottish Parliament is responsible for a wide range of powers such as education, health, housing, refuse collection, social work and local government. Children go to nursery, then primary school, followed by secondary. Some then go on to university. We all make use of our health services including visits to the doctors.

Comment

This is a very weak answer with basic exemplification. No marks for first sentence. Some basic information is given for education and health, each worth 1 mark. Overall this answer is a fail: 2/6.

What can we do to improve Answer 1? One approach is shown below.

ANSWER 2: Scottish Parliament

One power granted to the Scottish Parliament is education. This means that the Scottish government is responsible for staffing and changes to what is taught. We have Curriculum for Excellence in Scotland, which is taught in all Scottish schools from nursery to secondary and we have a different exam system from the rest of the UK. The Scottish Government at present is giving schools in challenging areas extra funding to try to raise standards.

A second power is health. This responsibility covers all aspects of health from doctors' surgeries to hospitals. Policies have been introduced to try to improve health and reduce health inequalities. Smoking is banned in public places and free prescriptions are available for all. In England many people, including students, have to pay for their prescriptions.

Comment

This answer provides detailed exemplification of both education and health. In education it covers Curriculum for Excellence and the financial help given to schools. In health it provides wide coverage of policies to reduce health inequalities. Overall, each description is worth 3 marks, so this answer gets 6/6.

ANSWER 3: UK Parliament

Two powers which the UK government is responsible for are defence and income tax. In defence the UK government is responsible for all the armed forces and the range of equipment available. The UK government makes the decision on whether to send troops abroad, as it did when it sent troops to Iraq. Recently the UK Government decided to renew the Trident nuclear programme. The Scottish Government does not support this decision but does not have the power to stop it.

The UK Government is responsible for the economy of the UK and sets the trade rules with other countries and organisations. All of the taxation decisions in the UK, such as income tax, are made by the UK Government.

Comment

The first paragraph is excellent. It describes, in detail, a range of UK responsibilities with up-to-date exemplification of the Trident nuclear programme – easily worth 3 marks. One mark is awarded for the first sentence of the second paragraph. The remaining information given is incorrect: income tax has been devolved to the Scottish Parliament since 2018. So overall this answer gets 4/6.

To improve this answer, a correct second power such as immigration should be chosen.

Now have a go at improving answer 3.

Test your knowledge and understanding: practice 'Describe' questions

MARKS

Democracy in Scotland and the UK

1 Committees have an important role in the Scottish Government.

Describe, **in detail**, **two** of the roles of committees in the Scottish Government.

4

2 The House of Lords has an important role in the UK Government.

Describe, **in detail**, **two** of the important roles of the House of Lords in the UK Government.

4

3 The Additional Member System (AMS) used to elect MSPs has many strengths.

Describe, **in detail**, **two** strengths of the Additional Member System (AMS).

6

4 The First-Past-the-Post System (FPTP) used to elect MPs has many strengths.

Describe, **in detail**, **two** strengths of the First-Past-the-Post System.

6

Social Issues in the UK: Social Inequality

5 Governments try to reduce social inequality.

Describe, **in detail**, **two** ways the Governments try to reduce social inequality in the UK.

6

6 There are many causes of social and economic inequality in the UK.

Describe, **in detail**, **two** causes of social and economic inequality in the UK.

4

Social Issues in the UK: Crime and the Law

7 Scotland has its own criminal courts.

Describe, **in detail**, **two** criminal courts in Scotland.

4

8 The work of the police in Scotland involves a variety of roles.

Describe, **in detail**, **two** roles of the police in Scotland.

6

MARKS

International Issues: World Powers

9 World Powers can have a military influence on other countries.

Describe, in **detail**, **two** ways the world power you have studied can have a military influence on other countries.

In your answer, you must state the world power you have studied.

4

10 All governments respond to a social inequality.

Describe, **in detail**, **two** ways the world power you have studied has responded to a social inequality.

In your answer, you must state the world power you have studied.

6

International Issues: World Issues

11 A range of social and economic factors are important causes of an international conflict or issue.

Describe, **in detail**, **two** socio-economic causes of an international conflict or issue you have studied.

In your answer, you must state the world issue you have studied.

4

12 Other countries are affected by international conflicts and issues in many different ways.

Describe, **in detail**, **two** ways other countries have been affected by an international conflict or issue.

In your answer, you must state the world issue you have studied.

6

Top Tip!

In your exam, the knowledge and skills questions for International Issues will not refer to a particular country or issue. You will be expected to base the 'describe' or 'explain' answer around your knowledge and understanding of the world power or world issue you have studied.

'Explain' questions

>> HOW TO ANSWER

These are the more challenging type of knowledge and understanding question, as your answer must go beyond simple description to provide reasons. 'Explain' questions are worth between 6 and 8 marks. Depending on the marks allocated, you will provide either two or three explanations.

For a 6- and 8-mark answer, you can be awarded up to 4 marks for an explanation which is relevant with exemplification. In an 8-mark answer you can receive credit for three explanations, but only two will be accepted for a 6-mark question.

Now look at an 'Explain' question and see what you need to do to get full marks:

Some victims of crime are affected more than others.

Explain, **in detail**, why some victims of crime are affected more than others.

> Hint!

Obviously, the consequences of crime impact on all its victims. Some groups, such as the elderly, may be affected more than others because of their vulnerability. Young people may feel more threatened by the gang and knife culture that might exist.

>> HOW TO ANSWER

ANSWER 1

Victims of crime may be any age or gender, and come from all neighbourhoods. They may experience theft or assaults and suffer from anxiety and a lack of security. Knife crime, especially in England, is a major problem for young people while it may not impact on older members of society. Again, if you are a victim of crime and live in a high crime area, you will feel more vulnerable and insecure than a person who lives in a more prosperous and safe area.

Comment

This is a very weak answer with basic exemplification. No marks for first sentence. Some basic information is given for linking knife crime to young people and the different neighbourhoods that people live in. So overall this answer is a fail: 2/6.

What this candidate needs to do is to really answer the question by choosing a group in society and explain why they may be more affected. Answer 2 concentrates on the elderly.

ANSWER 2

Victims of crime may be any age or gender, and come from all neighbourhoods. The elderly are especially more vulnerable and can suffer devastating consequences because they tend to be more frail and can be easy victims of mugging and injuries. They are regarded as an easy target because they may not be able to put up much of a struggle. Even in their own homes the elderly are not safe. Some may be in a confused state and are more likely to be the target of internet fraud or be taken in by 'cowboy' builders and tradespeople. The impact of crime can be devastating for the elderly and some may be too afraid to leave their home.

According to the annual Scottish Crime and Justice survey, property crime causes the most annoyance, followed by violent crimes. Victims also reported experiencing shock and anger.

Comment

The first paragraph of this answer provides a detailed explanation of why the elderly may be more affected. It highlights their frailty and vulnerability to a range of crimes – so this excellent answer would be worth 4 marks. The second paragraph provides interesting official statistics but is not relevant, so gets no marks. Overall 4/6.

To improve this answer and gain full marks, the candidate should choose another group that is more affected by crime, for example young people or people living in poorer areas, as outlined below.

ANSWER 3

Victims of crime may be any age or gender, and come from all neighbourhoods. The elderly are especially more vulnerable and can suffer devastating consequences because they tend to be more frail and can be easy victims of mugging and injuries. They are regarded as an easy target because they may not be able to put up much of a struggle. Even in their own homes the elderly are not safe. Some may be in a confused state and are more likely to be the target of internet fraud or be taken in by 'cowboy' builders and tradespeople. The impact of crime can be devastating for the elderly and some may be too afraid to leave their home.

According to official figures, if you live in the poorest 15% of areas, you are more likely to be a victim of crime and also more likely to be a repeat victim. People in these areas can be more affected if their house is burgled. They may not be able to afford house insurance. In contrast, wealthier householders will have house insurance and will not suffer any financial loss. Again, in areas of high crime, home insurance can be very expensive.

Comment

This paragraph explains why those who live in poorer areas are more likely to be affected by crime and uses the example of their house being burgled. Three marks awarded. The maximum overall is 6, so 6/6.

Test your knowledge and understanding: practice 'Explain' questions

Democracy in Scotland and the UK

MARKS

13 People in Scotland can participate in society in many ways.

Explain, **in detail**, **two** reasons why some people participate in one of the following:

a) Pressure groups

b) Trade unions.

OR

People in the United Kingdom can participate in society in many ways.

Explain, **in detail**, **two** reasons why some people participate in one of the following:

a) Pressure groups

b) Trade unions.

6

6

14 Women are under-represented in the Scottish Parliament.

Explain, **in detail**, **two** reasons why women are under-represented in the Scottish Parliament.

6

15 Women are under-represented in the UK Parliament.

Explain, **in detail**, **two** reasons why women are under-represented in the UK Parliament.

6

Social Issues in the UK – Social Inequality

16 Social and economic inequality has widened in recent years.

Explain, **in detail**, **two** reasons why social and economic inequality has widened in recent years.

6

17 Choose one of the groups below. You should state the group in your answer.

8

Groups in society that experience social and economic inequality			
Elderly people	Women	Ethnic minorities	People with disabilities

Explain, **in detail**, why the group you have chosen experiences social and economic inequality.

You should give a **maximum** of **three** reasons in your answer.

Social Issues in the UK: Crime and the Law

18 Social factors are a cause of crime in the UK.

Explain, **in detail**, **two** reasons why social factors are a cause of crime in the UK.

6

19 Prisons are an effective punishment for offenders guilty of serious crimes.

Explain, **in detail**, why prisons are an effective punishment for offenders guilty of serious crimes.

You should give a **maximum** of **three** reasons in your answer.

8

International Issues: World Powers

20 Some groups in society are poorly represented in government.

Explain, **in detail**, why some groups in society are poorly represented in government.

You should give a **maximum** of **three** reasons in your answer.

8

21 Some people think that government has been ineffective in tackling social inequality.

Explain, **in detail**, **two** reasons why some people think that government has been ineffective in tackling social inequality.

In your answer you must state the world power you have studied.

6

International Issues: World Issues

22 Political factors are important causes of international conflict and issues.

Explain, **in detail**, why political factors are important causes of international conflict and issues.

You should give a **maximum** of **three** reasons in your answer.

In your answer you must state the world issue you have studied.

8

23 Some people believe that international organisation(s) have had limited success in tackling world issues and conflicts.

Explain, **in detail**, **two** reasons why some people think that international organisation(s) have limited success in tackling a world issue or conflict you have studied.

In your answer you must state the world issue or conflict you have studied.

8

The evaluation of sources questions

The three types of questions here are:

▶ Using a range of sources of information to give detailed justifications for decisions

▶ Using a range of sources of information to support and oppose views

▶ Using a range of sources of information to give detailed support for valid conclusions.

Top Tip! There is now only ONE evaluation of sources question in each of the three sections. So, in the *Social Issues in the UK* section, you may have studied Crime and the Law, but the question may be about social inequality issues. It is your evaluation of sources skills that are being tested – no knowledge is required.

Tips for success	Things to avoid
Only use the sources provided.	Don't state your own knowledge or opinion on the topic.
Use all the sources provided and link evidence from different sources to give a detailed argument.	Don't just rely on one piece of evidence from a source to provide argument.
Interpret any statistical evidence to show how it links to the question being asked.	Don't just repeat the statistics without interpreting and explaining them.

Top Tip! If you only give evidence to justify your decision, the maximum mark you can receive is 8/10.

Justify a decision/recommendation questions

>> HOW TO ANSWER

Justify a decision/recommendation questions require you to select evidence from a range of sources in order to make and justify a decision/recommendation.

After reading the information you will decide which option or recommendation you will make. Either option is equally valid as there is balanced evidence to support either choice.

You should write at the beginning of your answer the option you have chosen, for example: 'I recommend Option 2'.

For each reason, you should write in separate paragraphs using detailed information from the sources to justify your decision.

You may decide to give three or four detailed reasons.

You should not forget to explain why you rejected the other option. Here you may wish to give one or two reasons.

Look at the question and answers below and see what you need to do to get full marks.

24 Study Sources 1, 2 and 3 then answer the question which follows.

The Scottish parliamentary constituency of Inverbank held a by-election in April 2016 to elect a new MP. You must decide who you would have chosen to be the party's candidate.

Option 1: Gemma Healy

Option 2: Lewis Elliot

SOURCE 1

Candidate Gemma Healy, social worker

Women are under represented across all senior management posts in the UK. We need to send out a political message that this must end. The best way to do this is for me to become our MP and a role model for all women.

I believe it is in our best interest for the UK to leave the EU and we should remember that the British people voted to leave. We pay too much into the EU and it is not working. EU countries which are using the euro, such as Greece, are in a mess.

I am totally against the UK having nuclear weapons and as such I am against the renewal of the Trident nuclear programme at the Faslane base on the Clyde. The billions of pounds being spent on it should be spent on education and health.

I am against the welfare cuts to public services being imposed by the UK Government. They will hit those on a low income the most. We must protect our families and prevent an increase in child poverty. However, I do not support pensioners getting a winter fuel allowance of £200 per household.

Candidate Lewis Elliot, local councillor

I support the renewal of the Trident nuclear programme at the Faslane base on the River Clyde as it will safeguard the jobs of those who work there. If the new Trident submarines are not built, unemployment will increase.

My priority is to fight against the savage welfare cuts being imposed on the most vulnerable and needy in our community. We need to protect our families and the elderly, and I support the payment of the winter fuel allowance.

We need to attract new jobs to the area to alleviate the high unemployment figures. Too many people are not in work and rely on state benefits to get by. If elected, I will work with Scottish Enterprise to achieve this.

I believe we should stay in the EU. I voted 'Yes' to remain in the EU in the referendum on EU membership. We are only a small island and we need the political and economic strength of the EU. The Scottish people voted to remain. We need to work together to resolve the migrant crisis.

SOURCE 2

Inverbank is a constituency for the UK Parliament in central Scotland. It is a former industrial town with a declining and ageing population. It has a proud industrial heritage, but the main employer now is a large call centre. The constituency is high in the deprivation index and the number of people using food banks has doubled in the last four years. Income deprivation is high. Average life expectancy in Inverbank is only 68 compared to the UK average of 80.

The party supports fairer gender representation in parliament and is in favour of positive discrimination. However, local party members believe that the choice of candidate should be based on experience and ability, and not just gender.

The number of skilled jobs in the area is declining. One important employer is the Ministry of Defence at the Trident Faslane base on the Clyde. A significant number of skilled and unskilled workers travel there every day. Michelle Daly, Chair of the Community Council, stated, 'Some constituents are very concerned about any decision not to renew Trident, as many will lose their jobs if the base is closed'.

Profile of Inverbank – key statistics (%)

	Inverbank	Scotland
Number of pensioners	13	10
Claiming benefits	20	15
School leavers with no qualifications	13	9
Experiencing long-term poor health	21	18
Visiting a food bank on a regular basis	9	6

SOURCE 3

Survey of public opinion in Inverbank (%)

	The Trident nuclear deterrent based at Faslane should be closed	The UK Parliament needs more female MPs	Welfare cuts impact most on the poor	The UK should remain in the EU
Strongly agree	20	23	24	20
Agree	32	38	48	44
Disagree	40	22	20	22
Strongly disagree	8	17	8	14

You must decide which option to recommend, either Gemma Healy (Option 1) or Lewis Elliot (Option 2).

MARKS

10

(i) Using Sources 1, 2 and 3, which option would you choose?

(ii) Give reasons to support your choice.

(iii) Explain why you did not choose the other option.

Your answer must be based on all **three** sources.

›› HOW TO ANSWER

ANSWER 1

I recommend Option 1: Gemma Healy.

Gemma Healy is the best candidate as she says that women are under-represented across all senior management posts and we need more women.

Comment

Only one piece of evidence from source 1 is used, so this answer gains only 1 mark.

The above answer can be improved by using a second source to support the evidence.

ANSWER 2

Gemma Healy is the best candidate as she says that women are under-represented across all senior management posts and we need more women. This is backed up in Source 3, which shows that public opinion in Inverbank agrees with her views.

Comment

An improved answer, as evidence is linked from Sources 1 and 3, and this is awarded 2 marks.

ANSWER 3

Gemma Healy is the best candidate as she says that women are under represented across all senior management posts and we need more women in important posts. She also states that one way to challenge under-representation is for her to become a role model female MP for all women. This is backed up in Source 3, which shows that a clear majority of Inverbank citizens agrees with her views.

Comment

An even better answer, as evidence is linked from Sources 1 and 3 with evaluative comment. This answer is awarded 3 marks.

Now it's your turn. Complete the rest of the answer to this question, then check your answer with the marking instructions on pages 32–33.

Test your evaluation of sources: practice 'Justify a decision' questions

25 Study Sources 1, 2 and 3 then answer the question which follows.

You have to choose which candidate you think would be the best choice as President of G20 country, Pimlico:

Option 1: Hilary Kennedy

Option 2: Ben Curtis

SOURCE 1

Factfile on Pimlico

Pimlico is a democratic nation that is a member of the G20. It is also a member of the United Nations. It has a population of 70 million and is considered to be one of the leading economies in the world.

Like many other countries, it has been in recession following the recent global economic crash. This has created rising prices and increased unemployment in the last few years. Some political leaders have tried to use the increased unemployment figures to restrict immigration to Pimlico. Immigration has never been a key election issue in Pimlico. Immigrants are seen as making a positive contribution to the cultural and economic life of Pimlico.

The government has had to introduce some charges for healthcare, which has caused a lot of anger and some demonstrations in the streets, particularly as the government has increased defence spending for the fourth year running. The plan to introduce charging for some types of healthcare remains deeply unpopular.

Pimlico has not been directly involved in the war on terror in Iraq, Afghanistan or Syria. It has not participated in any aerial bombing or offered armed forces personnel. Unlike other nations, Pimlico hasn't been the target of any terrorist attacks.

Pimlico's main area of employment used to be heavy industry such as coal mining and shipbuilding. Since the decline of these types of industries, Pimlico has built its financial services sector by attracting many international companies. The financial services sector employs just under a million workers but still has room for growth.

Tourism continues to be a major employer, contributing to just over 800,000 full-time and part-time jobs. The creation of a new high-speed train line prior to the recession has opened up many new markets and tourist destinations.

Despite growth in some areas, unemployment remains a key issue.

Crime rates are fairly low in Pimlico compared to other G20 countries. However, there has been an increase in some violent crime as well as property crime recently. Cybercrime has also risen but, generally speaking, Pimlico is a safe place to live.

SOURCE 2 Candidates' statements

Hilary Kennedy, Freedom Party

This election is an important one for our nation. It is one in which we have to make the right choices – the right choices for our economy. If elected, I will guarantee that I will look after and grow our economy. I will create jobs – safe, secure jobs in banking – by attracting the biggest banks and insurance companies to Pimlico.

I'll also stop the introduction of charges for our healthcare. The health of our nation is far too important to attach a price tag to. Healthcare should be based on need. If elected, I'll make sure that free healthcare remains exactly that.

I know that voters are worried about terrorism and want to see me do something about it. And rightly so. The safety and security of our citizens is our key objective and, if elected, I will protect the people of Pimlico from the very real threat of terrorism.

Vote Hilary!

Ben Curtis, Liberty Party

We have had a tough couple of years. Our economy went into recession and we are only beginning to see the green shoots of recovery. We need to focus on all areas of the economy, however the key to the future success of Pimlico is based on tourism not terrorism. If elected, I will put tourism as the key focus of our economic strategy.

We also need to tackle crime in our cities. Some crime figures are growing and I know that it is a concern of voters. Feeling safe in our cities is as important to me as it is to you. I will put more police on the streets to protect you and your property.

I will be tough on immigration. I will make it harder for immigrants to come to Pimlico. We welcome their contribution but enough is enough. Increased immigration costs real jobs and I will introduce a cap on the number of immigrants while we are still in recession. I will review this passport to Pimlico policy once the recession is over.

Vote Ben!

SOURCE 3

Opinion poll on voters' main election priorities. Question: What issues are important in the Pimlico presidential election?

Issue	Yes	No
Health	65%	35%
Jobs	92%	8%
Immigration	22%	78%
Defence	67%	33%
Economy	86%	14%
Law and order	61%	39%
Terrorism	31%	69%
Tourism	78%	22%

You must decide which option to recommend, either Hilary Kennedy (Option 1) or Ben Curtis (Option 2).

(i) Using Sources 1, 2 and 3, which option would you choose?

(ii) Give reasons to support your choice.

(iii) Explain why you did not choose the other option.

Your answer must be based on all **three** sources.

Opposing and supporting a view questions

>> HOW TO ANSWER

Supporting and opposing a view questions ask you to evaluate a limited range of sources, giving developed arguments supporting and opposing a view.

▶ You should make it clear whether you are supporting or opposing the viewpoint. This can be done by dividing your answer into 'Evidence to support' (reasons given) followed by 'Evidence to oppose' (reasons given).

Top Tip!

If you only provide evidence for and not against, or vice-versa, the maximum mark you can achieve is 6/10.

26 Study sources 1, 2 and 3 and then answer the question which follows.

SOURCE 1

Facts and viewpoints about zero-hours contracts

A zero-hours contract is a form of employment contract under which an employer does not have to state how many hours the employee will work per week. This means employees work only when they are needed by their employer. They will only be paid for the hours they work, so an employee may work only 15 hours in one week but 30 hours the following week.

This type of work contract is being used increasingly by UK employers. In 2015 the figure stood at an estimated 900,000 compared to 650,000 in 2013.

Well-known companies such as McDonald's and Sports Direct use these contracts, as do the NHS and charities. Zero-hours contracts are more common among young people than other age groups, with 37% of those employed on such contracts aged between 16 and 24.

Viewpoint of Michelle Kelly: retired clerical assistant

Although retired, I am working part-time on a zero-hours contract which gives me flexibility and keeps me active. I can spend time with my grandchildren and the income I receive allows me to have a better standard of living. I work alongside some university students who can combine their studies with some work and income. My employer is happy with this arrangement, and I am in control of my work–life balance, so I am happy to have a zero-hours contract.

Viewpoint of Sam Gunn: hotel worker

I am on a zero-hours contract and I feel I am being exploited by my employer. My contract effectively stops me from taking a second job even if it's clear I will have only eight hours in the coming week, as my contract states that I must be available at all times. These contracts mean employers avoid redundancy pay and pension contributions. I would prefer guaranteed weekly hours so that I can plan my finances. Some months I have to use food banks and take out payday loans with very high interest rates.

SOURCE 2

Survey findings of employment satisfaction – zero-hours and non-zero-hours workers (2014)		
	Zero-hours contract	**Non-zero-hours contract**
Satisfied with job	45%	57%
Work–life balance	65%	58%
Prefer more hours	50%	10%

SOURCE 3

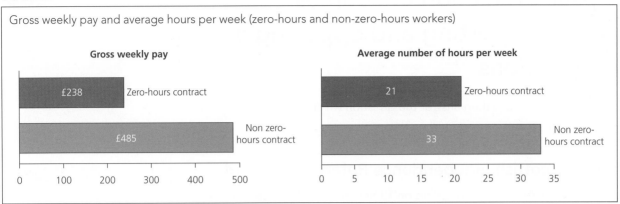

Gross weekly pay and average hours per week (zero-hours and non-zero-hours workers)

Gross weekly pay

- £238 — Zero-hours contract
- £485 — Non zero-hours contract

Average number of hours per week

- 21 — Zero-hours contract
- 33 — Non zero-hours contract

Using Sources 1, 2 and 3, give reasons to support and oppose the view of Ryan Willis:

> Zero-hours contract workers are exploited by their employers.
>
> View of Ryan Willis

MARKS

10

In your answer you must:

▶ give evidence from the sources that support Ryan Willis' view

and

▶ give evidence from the sources that oppose Ryan Willis' view.

Your answer must be based on all **three** sources.

≫ HOW TO ANSWER

Evidence to support the view

ANSWER 1

Sam Gunn, a hotel worker on a zero-hours contract, is unhappy; he feels he is being exploited by his employer.

Comment

Only one piece of evidence from Source 1 is used and so this only gains 1 mark.

The above answer could be improved by using information to explain why Sam is unhappy.

ANSWER 2

Sam Gunn, who is a hotel worker on a zero-hours contract, is unhappy as he feels he is being exploited by his employer. He might only work eight hours in a week as he is not guaranteed set working hours, but he is not allowed to take another job.

Comment

An improved answer, as it uses further detail from Source 1 to explain why Sam feels exploited. This answer is awarded 2 marks.

ANSWER 3

Sam Gunn, who is a hotel worker on a zero-hours contract, is unhappy as he feels he is being exploited by his employer. He might only work eight hours in a week as he is not guaranteed set working hours, but he is not allowed to take another job. He is not alone, as according to the survey in Source 2, one in every two workers on these contracts would prefer more hours.

Comment

An even better answer, as evidence links information from Sources 1 and 2 with evaluative comment. This answer is awarded 3 marks.

Now it's your turn to complete the rest of the answer above. Then check your answer with the marking instructions on pages 34–35.

Test your evaluation of sources: practice 'supporting and opposing a view' questions

27 Study Sources 1, 2 and 3 then answer the question which follows.

SOURCE 1

> ## Factfile on Scottish Independence Referendum 2014
>
> The Independence Referendum was held on 18 September 2014. Voters were asked, 'Should Scotland be an independent country?'
>
> The 'Yes' campaign was led by Alex Salmond and Nicola Sturgeon, the 'No' by Jim Murphy and Alistair Darling.
>
> Both campaigns were split along party political lines. The 'No' campaign was supported by Labour, the Conservatives and the Liberal Democrats, the 'Yes' by the SNP and the Green Party. Social media was used extensively by both sides, as was old media in the form of street rallies and speakers on empty upturned crates.
>
> Throughout the campaign the main issues were to do with the economic impact if Scotland was to become independent, including future oil revenues and what currency would be used if independence occurred.
>
> Over 4 million voters were eligible to vote. On the day, 3.6 million people turned out to vote. Just under 85 per cent of voters who could vote, did.
>
> The result saw the 'No' campaign victorious, winning just over 55 per cent of the vote compared to the 'Yes' campaign's total of just under 45 per cent. In terms of actual votes, the 'No' campaign achieved 2 million votes. The 'Yes' campaign totalled 1.6 million.
>
> The counting of the votes was via the 32 Scottish council areas. The 'No' campaign won 28 of these areas compared to only 4 for 'Yes'.

SOURCE 2

> ## Selected campaign views
>
> **'No' voter:**
>
> It was a hard-fought campaign. A very hard battle but our arguments about keeping Scotland part of the UK were strongest and we managed to convince the voters that we were right about being 'better together'. An excellent campaign was led by Jim Murphy saying 'No Thanks' to independence. Our arguments on the costs of independence, what currency we would use and economic uncertainty echoed with voters all over Scotland. The final result? Twenty-eight areas voted 'No'. Only four voted 'Yes'. You can't argue with that. A clear victory for 'No'.
>
> **'Yes' voter:**
>
> It was a hard-fought campaign. I thought 'Yes' did very well to engage so many younger voters. We ran the 'No' campaign close and at one stage we were even ahead in the opinion polls. The campaign energised many new voters and the way the 'Yes' campaign engaged with voters on social media shows that there are many positives to take out of this referendum result. It was good that Glasgow, the biggest city in Scotland, voted 'Yes' and shows that our message got across to some, but sadly not enough, voters. However, the 55 per cent 'No' to 45 per cent 'Yes' margin was a lot narrower than many people were predicting a year before the vote.

SOURCE 3

Selected referendum statistics

How Scotland's four main cities voted

City	Yes	No
Dundee	57%	43%
Glasgow	53.5%	46.5%
Edinburgh	39%	61%
Aberdeen	41%	59%

Voting by age

Age	16–24	25–34	35–44	45–54	54–64	65+
Yes	51%	59%	53%	52%	43%	27%
No	49%	41%	47%	48%	57%	63%

Voting by selected council area

Area	Yes	No
Dumfries	34%	66%
Orkney	33%	67%
North Ayrshire	49%	51%
Inverclyde	49.92%	50.08%
East Renfrewshire	37%	63%
Highland	47%	53%
Shetland	36%	64%
Falkirk	47%	53%
West Dunbartonshire	54%	46%

Using Sources 1, 2 and 3, give reasons to support and oppose the views of Bruce Hart.

MARKS
10

> The Scottish Independence Referendum was a massive disappointment for the 'Yes' campaign.
>
> *View of Bruce Hart*

In your answer you must:

▶ give evidence from the sources that support Bruce Hart's view

and

▶ give evidence from the sources that oppose Bruce Hart's view.

Your answer must be based on all **three** sources.

Test your evaluation of sources: Practice 'support for valid conclusions' questions

>> HOW TO ANSWER

Support for valid conclusions questions require you to use a range of sources and draw valid conclusions from them with supporting evidence.

After reading the information you should copy out one statement at a time and state your conclusion with relevant evidence from the relevant sources, before moving on to the next statement.

Top Tip!

For full marks you must give four developed conclusions.

28 Study Sources 1, 2 and 3 then answer the question which follows.

SOURCE 1

US presidential elections

Elections for president are held every four years. President Obama, the Democratic Party candidate who won both the 2008 and 2012 elections, could not stand again in 2016. The Democratic candidate for 2016 was Hillary Clinton, and for the Republicans, Donald Trump.

The president of the USA is not chosen directly by the US people. The Electoral College elects the president. Each state receives a set number of Electoral College votes depending on its population size. For example, Florida, with a large population, receives 29 Electoral College votes compared to the 3 received by Vermont, which has a small population.

There are 538 Electoral College votes in total. Citizens in each state vote for their respective presidential candidates. The candidate with the most votes in, say Florida, wins all of the Electoral College votes of that state.

In the 2012 presidential election, Obama was re-elected president. He received over 65 million votes compared to the Republican candidate, Mitt Romney, who won 61 million votes. In the Electoral College, Obama won 332 votes compared to the Republican candidate who won 206.

The outcome of the 2016 presidential election was an unexpected victory for the Republican candidate, Donald Trump, over Hillary Clinton, the Democrat candidate. He won 306 electoral college votes to Clinton's 232.

Yet Hillary Clinton won the popular vote (the total number of votes each candidate received across the country). Clinton won 65.5 million votes compared to Trump's 62.8 million votes.

In the 2016 election, the young, poorer groups and those from an ethnic minority background tended to support Clinton, while older and white voters tended to favour Trump.

SOURCE 2

US presidential election results 2012 and 2016

Party and candidate	Popular vote 2016	Popular vote 2012
Democrat: Clinton	48.1%	51.0%
Republican: Trump	46.2%	47.1%

Party and candidate	Electoral College 2016	Electoral College 2012
Democrat: Clinton	43.2%	61.7%
Republican: Trump	56.8%	38.3.%

Note: Obama was the Democrat candidate and Romney the Republican candidate in 2012.

SOURCE 3

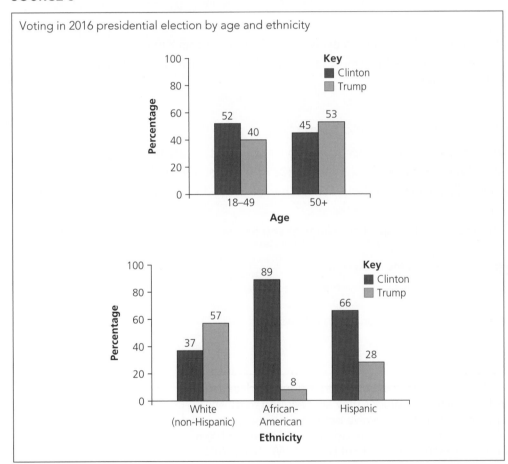

Voting in 2016 presidential election by age and ethnicity

Using Sources 1, 2 and 3, what **conclusions** can be drawn about the 2012 US presidential election?

You should reach a conclusion about **each** of the following:

▶ The Electoral College results of 2016 compared to 2012.

▶ The popular vote results of 2016 compared to 2012.

▶ The link between age and voting behaviour in the 2016 election.

▶ The link between ethnicity and voting behaviour in the 2016 election.

Your conclusions **must** be supported by evidence from the sources. You should link information within and between the sources in support of your conclusions.

Your answer must be based on all **three** sources.

MARKS

10

>> HOW TO ANSWER

ANSWER 1

The link between age and voting behaviour in the 2016 election.

Conclusion: Elderly people are more likely to vote for Trump and younger voters are more likely to vote for Clinton.

Comment

A conclusion is given for this answer. It fails to provide evidence and so would gain 1 mark for a valid conclusion.

ANSWER 2

The link between age and voting behaviour in the 2016 election.

Conclusion: Elderly people are more likely to vote for Trump and younger voters are more likely to vote for Clinton.

Those over the age of 50 favour Trump, while those under 50 are more likely to vote for Clinton.

Comment

A conclusion is given for this answer with supporting evidence and so would gain 2 marks.

So, what do you need to do to gain 3 marks? You must make use of the evidence provided to make evaluative comment, as outlined below.

ANSWER 3

The link between age and voting behaviour in the 2016 election.

Conclusion: Elderly people are more likely to vote for Trump and younger voters are more likely to vote for Clinton. There is a clear age divide in voting. Those over the age of 50 favoured Trump with an eight-point difference. In contrast, among the under-50 voters, Clinton had an even wider margin of a 12-point lead.

Comment

A conclusion is given for this answer with supporting evidence and evaluative comment and so it would gain 3 marks.

Now it's your turn to complete the rest of the answer above.

29 Study Sources 1, 2 and 3 then answer the question which follows.

SOURCE 1

The Department for Work and Pensions (DWP) can impose sanctions on claimants who are deemed to have failed to fulfil the conditions they are required to satisfy in order to receive their benefit payment. Sanctions involve benefit claimants losing all or a proportion of their benefit amount for a certain period of time. There has been an increase in the number of benefit sanctions carried out by the DWP. Since 2010 the rate of benefit sanctions has doubled. This has led to many individuals turning to food banks for assistance and help.

Food banks offer users a mix of services with donations often coming from members of the public. Many football clubs and local councils have organised food bank collections. Benefits issues such as benefit changes and delays to payments are often the reasons why many individuals are referred to food banks. Many food banks are staffed by volunteers and are often organised by local churches, mosques or community groups. The Trussell Trust is the UK's largest provider of food banks.

SOURCE 2

Causes of referrals to food banks

Benefit delays	34.6%
Low income	22.2%
Benefit changes	19.5%
Debt	7.2%
Homelessness	4.9%
Other	11.6%

Food aid provision across eight locations

Location	Total	Providing food parcels	Providing hot food
Glasgow	35	26	27
Dundee	12	3	9
Inverness	1	1	0
Fort William	1	1	0
Stirling	2	1	1
Falkirk	2	1	1
Kirriemuir	1	1	0
Forfar	1	1	0

SOURCE 3

Number of people given three-day emergency food parcels by
Trussell Trust food banks since 2010

2010–11	61,488
2011–12	128,697
2012–13	146,992
2013–14	913,138
2014–15	1,084,604

Using Sources 1, 2 and 3, what **conclusions** can be drawn about food banks?

You should reach a conclusion about each of the following:

▶ Benefits issues and referrals to food banks.

▶ Benefit sanctions and the use of food banks since 2010.

▶ Food banks and the services provided by them.

▶ The number of people given three-day emergency food parcels.

Your conclusions **must** be supported by evidence from the sources. You should link information within and between the sources in support of your conclusions.

Your answer must be based on all **three** sources.

10

Test your knowledge and understanding: answers to 'Describe' questions

1 Committees have an important role in the Scottish Government.

Describe, **in detail**, **two** of the roles of committees in the Scottish Government.

You can be credited in a number of ways **up to a maximum of 4 marks**.

Possible approaches to answering the question:

There are 15 committees in the Scottish Parliament, with most having between 7 and 11 MSPs.

1 mark – accurate but undeveloped point.

There are 15 committees in the Scottish Parliament, with most having between 7 and 11 MSPs. Each committee is responsible for a particular area or subject such as Education and Skills.

2 marks – accurate point with development.

There are 15 committees in the Scottish Parliament, with most having between 7 and 11 MSPs. Each committee is responsible for a particular area or subject such as Education and Skills. Committees are expected to scrutinise government proposals and can propose amendments.

3 marks – accurate point with development and exemplification.

Credit reference to aspects of the following:

▶ Committees play an important role as there is no second chamber like the House of Lords in Westminster.

▶ Committees can investigate key aspects of their remit.

▶ Membership and convenorship reflect the balance of political power within Parliament as a whole.

▶ Scrutiny is a crucial role. All government bills must go through the committees and amendments can be made.

▶ Two types of committees, mandatory and subject, can conduct inquiries and invite expert witnesses.

2 The House of Lords has an important role in the UK Government.

Describe, **in detail**, **two** of the important roles of the House of Lords in the UK Government.

You can be credited in a number of ways **up to a maximum of 4 marks**.

Possible approaches to answering the question:

The House of Lords can examine in detail Government legislation.

1 mark – accurate but undeveloped point.

The House of Lords can examine Government legislation. It can propose amendments and improvements to Government bills and perhaps win popular support for its proposals.

2 marks – accurate point with development.

The House of Lords can examine government legislation. It can propose amendments and improvements to Government bills and perhaps win popular support for its proposals. If the Government rejects their proposals, the Lords can, if it is not a money bill, delay it for a year.

3 marks – accurate point with development and exemplification.

Credit reference to aspects of the following:

▶ Discuss laws in depth and advise the Government.

▶ Bring expertise to debates.

▶ Can delay legislation.

▶ May be able to force Government to rethink legislation.

▶ Can bring ministers into Government.

3 The Additional Member System (AMS) used to elect MSPs has many strengths.

Describe, **in detail**, **two** strengths of the Additional Member System (AMS).

You can be credited in a number of ways **up to a maximum of 6 marks**.

Possible approaches to answering the question:

AMS provides greater representation for very small parties such as the Greens.

1 mark – accurate but undeveloped point.

AMS provides greater representation for very small parties such as the Greens. In every election since 1999, the Green Party has had representation in the Parliament.

2 marks – accurate point with development.

AMS provides greater representation for very small parties such as the Greens. In every election since 1999, the Green Party has had representation in the Scottish Parliament. Having two votes enables voters to vote for another party for their regional vote. For example, you can vote SNP or Labour as your constituency MSP and the Greens for your Regional representative.

3 marks – accurate point with development and exemplification.

Credit reference to aspects of the following:

▶ AMS is fair because it produces a close correlation between the share of the votes and the share of seats.

▶ In the 2016 Scottish Parliament elections Labour won 21% of the votes and just under 20% of the seats.

▶ Provides wider choice as voters have two votes.

▶ It is argued that AMS reduces the number of 'wasted votes'.

4 The First-Past-the-Post System (FPTP) used to elect MPs has many strengths.

Describe, **in detail**, **two** strengths of the First-Past-the-Post System

You can be credited in a number of ways **up to a maximum of 6 marks**.

Possible approaches to answering the question:

FPTP usually provides a strong single-party government that can implement its election manifesto.

1 mark – accurate but undeveloped point.

FPTP usually provides a strong single-party government that can implement its election manifesto. In the 2015 General Election, David Cameron won with a clear majority and could get his legislation through Parliament.

2 marks – accurate point with development.

FPTP usually provides a strong single-party government that can implement its election manifesto. In the 2015 General Election, David Cameron won with a clear majority and could get his legislation through Parliament. In their 2015 election manifesto, the Conservatives promised to hold a referendum on UK membership of the EU.

3 marks – accurate point with development and exemplification.

Credit reference to aspects of the following:

▶ FPTP prevents extremist parties from obtaining representation.

▶ The party with the most votes usually wins a majority of seats and can implement their policies.

▶ It provides a strong link between constituents and MP.

▶ It usually avoids coalition or minority government and prevents smaller parties influencing government policies.

5 Governments try to reduce social inequality.

Describe, **in detail**, **two** ways the Governments try to reduce social inequality in the UK.

You can be credited in a number of ways **up to a maximum of 6 marks**.

Possible approaches to answering the question:

One way that Government has tried to tackle social inequality is by introducing the Equality Act.

1 mark – accurate but undeveloped point.

One way that Government has tried to tackle social inequality is by introducing the Equality Act. This protects people from being discriminated against because of their gender, age and other characteristics.

2 marks – accurate with development.

One way that Government has tried to tackle social inequality is by introducing the Equality Act. This protects people from being discriminated against because of their gender, age and other characteristics. It makes sure that men and women get paid the same for doing work of equal value such as a school janitor and school cleaner.

3 marks – accurate point with development and exemplification.

Credit reference to aspects of the following:

▶ Welfare reforms since 2010, such as Universal Credit, PIP and freezing of benefits.

▶ National Minimum Wage/National Living Wage.

▶ Free prescriptions and eye tests in Scotland.

▶ Equality Act and EHRC.

▶ Health promotions and campaigns.

You can make reference to social inequalities such as health inequalities, wealth inequalities, inequalities between groups differentiated by gender, race etc.

---

6 There are many causes of social and economic inequality in the UK.

Describe, **in detail**, **two** causes of social and economic inequality in the UK.

You can be credited in a number of ways **up to a maximum of 4 marks**.

Possible approaches to answering the question:

One cause of inequality is the low income that many families and individuals receive.

1 mark – accurate but undeveloped point.

One cause of inequality is the low income that many families and individuals receive. They might be in work, but it might be on a zero-hours contract which can pay a low wage and put families below the official poverty line.

2 marks – accurate with development.

One cause of inequality is the low income that many families and individuals receive. They might be in work, but it might be on a zero-hours contract which can pay a low wage and put families below the official poverty line. A Joseph Rowntree Foundation (JRF) report stated that 14 million people live in poverty – more than one in five of the population.

3 marks – accurate point with development and exemplification.

Credit reference to aspects of the following:

▶ Employment/unemployment.

▶ Income.

▶ Educational attainment.

▶ Discrimination.

▶ Fuel poverty.

▶ Welfare reforms of the Conservative Party.

---

7 Scotland has its own criminal courts.

Describe, **in detail**, **two** criminal courts in Scotland.

You can be credited in a number of ways **up to a maximum of 4 marks**.

Possible approaches to answering the question:

The High Court is the supreme criminal court in Scotland and deals with the most serious crimes.

1 mark – accurate but undeveloped point.

The High Court is the supreme criminal court in Scotland and deals with the most serious crimes, such as murder. The custodial sentencing powers of this court are unlimited.

2 marks – accurate with development.

The High Court is the supreme criminal court in Scotland and deals with the most serious crimes, such as murder. The custodial sentencing powers of this court are unlimited for crimes such as murder. All cases held here have a jury of 15 members, and a majority of 8 is needed to achieve a verdict.

3 marks – accurate point with development and exemplification.

Credit reference to aspects of the following:

▶ High Court – supreme court of Scotland and deals with the most serious of crimes.

▶ Sheriff Court – can impose custodial or non-custodial sentences and can refer to the High Court.

▶ Justice of the Peace Court – deals with minor offences and can impose short-term prison sentences and non-custodial sentences.

8   The work of the police in Scotland involves a variety of roles.

     Describe, **in detail**, **two** roles of the police in Scotland.

     You can be credited in a number of ways **up to a maximum of 6 marks**.

Possible approaches to answering the question:

One role of the police is to maintain law and order in society.

1 mark – accurate but undeveloped point.

One role of the police is to maintain law and order. They achieve this by working on crime prevention by maintaining a presence in the community.

2 marks – accurate point with development.

One role of the police is to maintain law and order. They achieve this by working on crime prevention by maintaining a presence in the community. The police will also visit schools and give presentations on issues such as knife crime and the dangers of drugs.

3 marks – accurate point with development and exemplification.

Credit reference to aspects of the following:

▶ Maintain law and order.

▶ Detect crimes, e.g. carry out investigations, interview witnesses, process evidence.

▶ Protection of the public, e.g. security at football matches.

▶ Initiatives, e.g. knife amnesties.

9   World Powers can have a military influence on other countries.

     Describe, **in detail**, **two** ways the world power you have studied can have a military influence on other countries.

     In your answer, you must state the world power you have studied.

     You can be credited in a number of ways **up to a maximum of 4 marks**.

Possible approaches to answering the question: the USA

The USA has a massive military presence and has troops and bases around the globe.

1 mark – accurate but undeveloped point.

The USA has a massive military presence and has troops and bases around the globe. Its aircraft carriers patrol the Asian seas to combat China's aggression.

2 marks – accurate point with development.

The USA has a massive military presence and has troops and bases around the globe. Its aircraft carriers patrol the Asian seas to combat China's aggression. Without the US military force, Taiwan would be vulnerable to an attack from China and a possible invasion.

3 marks – accurate point with development and exemplification.

Credit reference to aspects of the following:

▶ the USA is the dominant member of NATO and contributes most of the budget.

▶ the USA's role as the world's 'policeman'.

▶ the USA's military presence in Europe, Middle East and Asia.

▶ US military spending accounts for 37% of global military spending.

10   All governments respond to a social inequality.

     Describe, **in detail**, **two** ways the world power you have studied has responded to a social inequality.

     In your answer, you must state the world power you have studied.

     You can be credited in a number of ways **up to a maximum of 6 marks**.

Possible approaches to answering the question: China

A social inequality is the disparity of spending and provision between urban and rural schools in China.

1 mark – accurate but undeveloped point.

A social inequality is the disparity of spending and provision between urban and rural schools in China. Tuition and book fees have now been abolished for primary and junior pupils, to enable poor rural children to stay on at school.

2 marks – accurate with development.

A social inequality is the disparity of spending and provision between urban and rural schools in China. Tuition and book fees have now been abolished for primary and junior pupils to enable poor rural children to stay on at school. To encourage rural children to finish high school, universities have increased their quota of rural students.

3 marks – accurate point with development and exemplification.

Credit reference to aspects of the following:

▶ More money to be spent on rural pupils. In 2014 annual expenditure for an urban pupil was 20,000 yuan, compared with just 3,000 yuan in a rural school.

▶ In 1999, fewer than 10% of rural pupils completed senior middle school; the figure now is around 40%.

▶ Tuition and book fees have been scrapped for primary and junior pupils.

▶ Coverage of health inequalities between urban and rural areas: migrant workers and urban citizens.

---

11 A range of social and economic factors are important causes of an international conflict or issue.

Describe, **in detail**, **two** socio-economic causes of an international conflict or issue you have studied.

In your answer, you must state the world issue you have studied.

You can be credited in a number of ways **up to a maximum of 4 marks**.

Possible approaches to answering the question: Terrorism

A group may resort to terrorism due to religious extremism.

1 mark – accurate but undeveloped point.

A group may resort to terrorism due to religious extremism. Islamist extremists such as members of IS strongly disagree with the Western way of life and the West's involvement in Arab countries.

2 marks – accurate point with development.

A group may resort to terrorism due to religious extremism. Islamist extremists such as members of IS strongly disagree with the Western way of life and the West's involvement in Arab countries. IS wants to create an Islamic state based upon an extreme version of sharia law.

3 marks – accurate point with development and exemplification.

Credit reference to aspects of the following:

▶ Poverty can radicalise many dispossessed people in countries such as Syria, Somalia, Nigeria and Iraq.

▶ Religious extremism and a rejection of Western values can lead to the creation of groups such as IS.

▶ Groups may feel that they are being discriminated against and may resort to terrorism in retaliation.

---

12 Other countries are affected by international conflicts and issues in many different ways.

Describe, **in detail**, **two** ways other countries have been affected by an international conflict or issue.

In your answer, you must state the world issue you have studied.

You can be credited in a number of ways **up to a maximum of 6 marks**.

Possible approaches to answering the question: Terrorism

International conflicts such as terrorism can cause high numbers of refugees in individual nations.

1 mark – accurate but undeveloped point.

International conflicts such as terrorism can cause high numbers of refugees in individual nations. The increase of terrorism in Syria has seen a huge number of refugees in countries such as Turkey as well as European nations such as Germany.

2 marks – accurate with development.

International conflicts such as terrorism can cause high numbers of refugees in individual nations. The increase of terrorism in Syria has seen a huge number of refugees in countries such as Turkey as well as European nations such as Germany. This has led to huge pressure being put on these countries' economies and has also led to tension within these countries.

3 marks – accurate point with development and exemplification.

Credit reference to aspects of the following:

▶ Effects of terrorism.

▶ Creates instability within your own country.

▶ Effects of mass migration.

▶ Pressure placed on government to provide humanitarian aid.

Test your knowledge and understanding: answers to 'Explain' questions

13 People in Scotland can participate in society in many ways.

Explain, **in detail**, **two** reasons why some people participate in one of the following:

a) Pressure groups

b) Trade unions.

OR

People in the United Kingdom can participate in society in many ways.

Explain, **in detail**, **two** reasons why some people participate in one of the following:

a) Pressure groups

b) Trade unions.

You can be credited in a number of ways **up to a maximum of 6 marks**.

Possible approaches to answering the question: Pressure groups

People join a pressure group because they have strong views on a local, national or international issue.

1 mark – accurate but undeveloped point.

People join a pressure group because they have strong views on a local, national or international issue. They wish to be involved in collective action to protect the environment through Greenpeace or local action to protest against President Trump's visit to Scotland.

2 marks – accurate with development.

People join a pressure group because they have strong views on a local, national or international issue. They wish to be involved in collective action to protect the environment through Greenpeace or local action to protest against President Trump's visit to Scotland. Joining a pressure group means lots of people campaign together so they have more of an impact. Greenpeace has around 130,000 members – this gives them strength in numbers and increases their collective influence on the government.

4 marks – accurate point with development analysis and exemplification.

Credit reference to aspects of the following:

▶ Collective action more effective than individual.

▶ Pressure groups have experience of campaigning and have financial resources.

▶ Believe strongly about an issue such as the environment or human rights.

▶ Can influence governments at different levels.

Possible approaches to answering the question: Trade unions

People join a trade union so that they can work together for better wages and employment conditions.

1 mark – accurate but undeveloped point.

People join a trade union so that they can work together for better wages and employment conditions. This is called collective bargaining and enables experienced trade union officials to negotiate with management on behalf of the workers.

2 marks – accurate with development.

People join a trade union so that they can work together for better wages and employment conditions. This is called collective bargaining and enables experienced trade union officials to negotiate with management on behalf of the workers. Over 6 million workers in the UK belong to a trade union – over 600,000 in Scotland. This gives them strength in numbers and increases their collective influence on employers and government.

4 marks – accurate point with development analysis and exemplification.

Credit reference to aspects of the following:

▶ Collective action more effective than individual.

▶ Protect rights at work, e.g. health and safety, pay, pensions.

▶ Trade unions have experience negotiating with management.

▶ Trade unions have legal teams you can use.

14 Women are under-represented in the Scottish Parliament.

Explain, in detail, **two reasons** why women are under-represented in the Scottish Parliament.

You can be credited in a number of ways **up to a maximum of 6 marks**.

Possible approaches to answering the question:

If the composition of the Scottish Parliament was based on the Scottish population, there would be around 63 female MSPs, not the 45 we have at present. (In 2003 there were 51 female MSPs.)

1 mark – accurate but undeveloped point.

If the composition of the Scottish Parliament was based on the Scottish population, there would be around 63 female MSPs, not the 45 we have at present. (In 2003 there were 51 female MSPs.) This under-representation can be explained by the historical dominance of men in politics and the harassment that female politicians receive.

2 marks – accurate with development.

If the composition of the Scottish Parliament was based on the Scottish population, there would be around 63 female MSPs, not the 45 we have at present. (In 2003 there were 51 female MSPs.) This under-representation can be explained by the historical dominance of men in politics and the harassment that female politicians receive. It is difficult in politics to maintain a work–home balance. A female candidate from Inverness with a young family has to consider that she will be working almost 200 miles away in Edinburgh, and might decide she prefers to work in her local area.

4 marks – accurate point with development analysis and exemplification.

Credit reference to aspects of the following:

▶ Historical male dominance of politics and difficult for women to break the glass ceiling.

▶ Parliament is a male-dominated environment and male representatives can try to dominate proceedings.

▶ Difficult to maintain a work–home balance, especially if the female MSP has a young family.

15 Women are under-represented in the UK Parliament.

Explain, **in detail**, two reasons why women are under-represented in the UK Parliament.

You can be credited in a number of ways **up to a maximum of 6 marks**.

Possible approaches to answering the question:

If the composition of the UK Parliament was based on the UK population, there would be around 320 female MPs, not the 208 we have at present. (In 2005 there were only 125 female MPs.)

1 mark – accurate but undeveloped point.

If the composition of the UK Parliament was based on the UK population, there would be around 320 female MPs, not the 208 we have at present. (In 2005 there were only 125 female MPs.) This under-representation can be explained by the historical dominance of men in politics and the harassment that female politicians receive.

2 marks – accurate with development.

If the composition of the UK Parliament was based on the UK population, there would around 320 female MPs, not the 208 we have at present. (In 2005 there were only 125 female MPs.) This under-representation can be explained by the historical dominance of men in politics and the harassment that female politicians receive. It is difficult in politics to maintain a work–home balance. A female candidate from Glasgow with a young family has to consider that she will be working around 600 miles away in London, and might decide she prefers to work in the local area.

4 marks – accurate point with development analysis and exemplification.

Credit reference to aspects of the following:

▶ Historical male dominance of politics and difficult for women to break the glass ceiling.

▶ Parliament is a male-dominated environment and male representatives can try to dominate proceedings.

▶ Difficult to maintain a work–home balance especially if the female MP has a young family.

16 Social and economic inequality has widened in recent years.

Explain, **in detail**, two reasons why social and economic inequality has widened in recent years.

You can be credited in a number of ways **up to a maximum of 6 marks**.

Possible approaches to answering the question:

The Joseph Rowntree Foundation (JRF) in its 2018 Report blamed the welfare reforms brought in by the Conservative Government.

1 mark – accurate but undeveloped point.

The Joseph Rowntree Foundation (JRF) in its 2018 Report blamed the welfare reforms brought in by the Conservative Government. Over the last 5 years a further 400,000 UK children have fallen into poverty because of the cuts to welfare payments.

2 marks – accurate with development.

The Joseph Rowntree Foundation (JRF) in its 2018 Report blamed the welfare reforms brought in by the Conservative Government. Over the last 5 years a further 400,000 UK children have fallen into poverty because of the cuts to welfare payments. The increase in child poverty can be linked to a freeze on benefits, a reduction in tax credits and stagnant wages for low-income families. In contrast, those earning over £150,000 have experienced no decline in their income.

4 marks – accurate point with development analysis and exemplification.

Credit reference to aspects of the following:

▶ Freezing of a wide range of benefits such as tax credits and child benefit.

▶ Growth of zero-hours contracts pushing workers into poverty.

▶ Increase in home utility charges leading to greater fuel poverty.

▶ Introduction of universal credits and harsh sanction rules.

17 Explain, in detail, why the group you have chosen experiences social and economic inequality.

You should give a **maximum** of **three** reasons in your answer.

You can be credited in a number of ways **up to a maximum of 8 marks**.

Possible approaches to answering the question: Women

Despite more women going through higher education than men, women still lag behind men in income and in promotion.

1 mark – accurate but undeveloped point.

Despite more women going through higher education than men, women still lag behind men in income and in promotion. Women are over-represented in areas of work that are low paid and are under-represented in highly paid senior-management posts.

2 marks – accurate with development.

Despite more women going through higher education than men, women still lag behind men in income and in promotion. Women are over-represented in areas of work that are low paid and are under-represented in highly paid senior-management posts. Women tend to bear the main responsibility for childcare and domestic work, and as such many are not able to work the long hours required for a promoted post.

3 marks – accurate point with development analysis and exemplification.

Credit reference to aspects of the following:

▶ Women over-represented in low-paid areas of the economy.

▶ Female-dominated occupations described as the five Cs: caring, cashiering, catering, cleaning and clerical occupations.

▶ Traditional role as unpaid carers.

▶ Impact of glass ceiling.

18 Social factors are a cause of crime in the UK.

Explain, **in detail**, **two** reasons why social factors are a cause of crime in the UK.

You can be credited in a number of ways **up to a maximum of 6 marks**.

Possible approaches to answering the question:

A major cause of crime is drug addiction.

1 mark – accurate but undeveloped point.

A major cause of crime is drug addiction. Drug addicts need to pay for their drugs and will steal to fund their habit.

2 marks – accurate point with development.

A major cause of crime is drug addiction. Drug addicts need to pay for their drugs and will steal to fund their habit. Statistics show that people with drug addiction are more likely to be arrested for crimes such as mugging, burglary and shoplifting.

3 marks – accurate point with development analysis and exemplification.

Credit reference to aspects of the following:

▶ Peer pressure/gang culture/family influence.

▶ Poverty/deprivation.

▶ Mental health and alcohol/drug abuse.

▶ Greed – white collar crime.

▶ Poor educational attainment.

19 Prisons are an effective punishment for offenders guilty of serious crimes.

Explain, **in detail**, why prisons are an effective punishment for offenders guilty of serious crimes.

You should give a **maximum** of **three** reasons in your answer.

You can be credited in a number of ways **up to a maximum of 8 marks**.

Possible approaches to answering the question:

At any one time over 90,000 UK criminals are locked up, many of whom are violent.

1 mark – accurate but undeveloped point.

At any one time over 90,000 UK criminals are locked up, many of whom are violent. This means that they are not a danger to the public.

2 marks – accurate point with development.

At any one time over 90,000 UK criminals are locked up, many of whom are violent. This means that they are not a danger to the public. Victims of serious crime would feel that if the offender was given a non-custodial punishment, justice had not been served. They might also be afraid that the violent criminal might come after them again and they might live in fear. The media and public would expect a custodial sentence to deter individuals from committing crime.

4 marks – accurate point with development analysis and exemplification.

Credit reference to aspects of the following:

▶ Prisons protect the public from dangerous criminals.

▶ Provide justice to the victims.

▶ Can deter criminals.

▶ Prisons provide opportunities to receive treatment if prisoners have drug or mental health issues.

▶ Provide appropriate punishment.

20 Some groups in society are poorly represented in government.

Explain, **in detail**, why some groups in society are poorly represented in government.

You should give a **maximum** of **three** reasons in your answer.

You can be credited in a number of ways **up to a maximum of 8 marks**.

Possible approaches to answering the question: China

Ethnic minorities in China are poorly represented in government.

1 mark – accurate but undeveloped point.

Ethnic minorities in China are poorly represented in government. The original citizens of Tibet and Xinjiang are not allowed to participate in the running of their province.

2 marks – accurate with development.

Ethnic minorities in China are poorly represented in government. The original citizens of Tibet and Xinjiang are not allowed to participate in the running of their province. The Communist leader of both provinces is always from the dominant ethnic group – the Han (around 95% of the population). It is dangerous for these ethnic minorities to get involved in politics as they will be arrested and placed in prison.

4 marks – accurate point with development analysis and exemplification.

Credit reference to aspects of the following:

▶ Any attempt to demand the vote or set up a political party will be severely punished.

▶ The Communist Party has a limited membership (around 6% of the population), so it is difficult to become involved.

▶ Ethnic minorities have no say in the running of their province.

21 Some people think that government has been ineffective in tackling social inequality.

Explain, **in detail**, **two** reasons why some people think that government has been ineffective in tackling social inequality.

In your answer you must state the world power you have studied.

You can be credited in a number of ways **up to a maximum of 6 marks**.

Possible approaches to answering the question: the USA

The USA does not have a state-funded national health service, and healthcare is expensive.

1 mark – accurate but undeveloped point.

The USA does not have a state-funded national health service, and healthcare is expensive. Health provision is provided mostly through private health insurance companies and not all patients get the treatment they need.

2 marks – accurate with development.

The USA does not have a state-funded national health service, and healthcare is expensive. Health provision is provided mostly through private health insurance companies and not all patients get the treatment they need. President Obama brought in the Affordable Care Act which made health insurance more accessible. Over 8 million extra Americans, many from ethnic minority communities, now have health cover. However, President Trump is trying to abolish the Affordable Care Act.

4 marks – accurate point with development analysis and exemplification.

Credit reference to aspects of the following:

▶ Educational inequalities.

▶ Income and employment inequalities.

▶ Housing inequalities.

▶ Health inequalities.

22 Political factors are important causes of international conflict and issue.

Explain, **in detail**, why political factors are important causes of international conflict and issues.

You should give a **maximum** of **three** reasons in your answer.

In your answer you must state the world issue you have studied.

You can be credited in a number of ways **up to a maximum of 8 marks**.

Possible approaches to answering the question: Under-development in Africa

Political factors such as corrupt governments and ethnic conflict are important causes of under-development.

1 mark – accurate but undeveloped point.

Political factors such as corrupt governments and ethnic conflict are important causes of under-development. Many African states are kleptocracies, where leaders use their power to benefit themselves by stealing public funds and/or aid money.

2 marks – accurate with development.

Political factors such as corrupt governments and ethnic conflict are important causes of under-development. Many African states are kleptocracies, where leaders use their power to benefit themselves by stealing public funds and/or aid money. Some also accept bribes. The late dictator of Nigeria stole around 2 billion dollars. This money could have been used to improve the health and wealth of Nigerian citizens.

4 marks – accurate point with development analysis and exemplification.

Credit reference to aspects of the following:

▶ Corrupt governments and abuse of power, for example Nigeria and Zimbabwe.

▶ Ethnic tension/conflict.

▶ Civil war, for example South Sudan.

▶ Political mismanagement.

23 Some people believe that international organisation(s) have had limited success in tackling world issues and conflicts.

Explain, **in detail**, **two** reasons why some people think that international organisation(s) have limited success in tackling a world issue or conflict you have studied.

In your answer you must state the world issue or conflict you have studied.

You can be credited in a number of ways **up to a maximum of 6 marks**.

Possible approaches to answering the question:

Some people believe that organisations such as the UN have had limited success in tackling issues such as poor health in the developing world. This is because despite some improvements poor health still exists.

1 mark – accurate but undeveloped point.

NATO sees one of its main roles as defeating international terrorism. It has had some success such as using drones to target IS leaders; however, attacks such as the two in Paris in 2015 show that terrorism hasn't fully been defeated.

2 marks – accurate point with development.

NATO sees one of its main roles as defeating international terrorism. It has had some success such as using drones to target IS leaders; however, attacks such as the two in Paris in 2015 show that terrorism hasn't fully been defeated. In the last four years the number of terrorist incidents across the world has trebled and parts of the world such as the Middle East have seen a big increase in terrorist attacks.

3 marks – accurate point with development, exemplification and analysis.

Credit reference to aspects of the following:

▶ The Democratic Republic of the Congo (DRC) – NATO has had success in parts of the DRC in ending civil war but has been a failure because much of the DRC is still in conflict and turmoil.

▶ Syria – the UN has been successful in feeding and housing refugees in neighbouring countries but has been a failure in being unable to agree collective action due to the Russian veto.

▶ Libya – the military power of NATO successfully deposed the dictatorship of Colonel Gaddafi but it has failed to make more progress in the country due to tribal/religious conflict.

Test your evaluation of sources: answers to 'Justify a decision' questions

24 You must decide which option to recommend, either Gemma Healy (Option 1) or Lewis Elliot (Option 2).

   (i) Using Sources 1, 2 and 3, which option would you choose?

   (ii) Give reasons to support your choice.

   (iii) Explain why you did not choose the other option.

   Your answer must be based on all **three** sources.

   You can be credited in a number of ways **up to a maximum of 10 marks.**

Possible approaches to answering the question:

For Option 1:

I would choose Gemma Healy as she has the experience of being a social worker and will know about the impact of welfare cuts.

1 mark – evidence drawn from Source 1.

In Source 1, Gemma Healy says that women are under-represented across all senior management posts and we need more women MPs. She is right as 61% of the Inverbank public agree with her.

2 marks – evaluative terminology with limited evidence.

In Source 1, Gemma Healy states that she is 'against the welfare cuts' and that they will impact on the most vulnerable and needy in the community. She is completely correct as Source 2 indicates that Inverbank has a high deprivation index with life expectancy only 68, well below the UK average of 80.

3 marks – detailed evidence drawn from two sources with evaluative terminology.

Credit reference to aspects of the following:

▶ Totally against the renewal of the Trident nuclear weapons programme, a waste of 'billions of pounds' and 52% of public opinion agree (Source 3).

▶ 'We pay too much into the EU and it is not working. Greece is in a mess.' (Source 1).

▶ The number of people using food banks has doubled in the last 4 years (Source 2).

▶ Deprivation impacts on health indicators, with Inverbank having a greater number of people experiencing long-term health problems (21% compared to 18%) (Source 2).

▶ Over 70% of public opinion agrees that welfare cuts impact on the poor (Source 3).

Against Option 1:

Gemma states that we should vote to leave the EU (Source 1) but Source 3 shows only 34% of the Inverbank public agree.

2 marks – evaluative terminology with limited evidence.

Credit reference to aspects of the following:

▶ Supports the closure of the nuclear base at Faslane on the Clyde (Source 1), however, the Community Council is against the closure of Faslane as many workers will lose their jobs (Source 2).

▶ Also in Source 2, there is already a significantly higher rate of unemployed people claiming benefits – 20% compared to the Scottish average of 15%.

▶ Gemma wants to end the winter fuel allowance, however, Inverbank has a higher number of pensioners compared to other parts of Scotland.

For Option 2:

I would choose Lewis Elliot as he has experience as a local councillor.

1 mark – evidence drawn from Source 1.

In Source 1, Lewis Elliot states that he will protect families and the elderly to maintain all their present benefits as poverty is an issue in Inverbank. He is right as the number of pensioners and those claiming benefits are significantly above the Scottish figures (Source 2).

2 marks – evidence drawn from Sources 1 and 2.

In Source 1, Lewis Elliot states that 'we need to attract new jobs to the area' and that too many people rely on state benefits to get by. He is correct as in Source 2 the percentage of people claiming benefits in Inverbank is higher than the Scottish figure (20% compared to 15%). The difference is significant and is worrying, especially for the school leavers with no qualifications (13% compared to 9%).

3 marks – detailed evidence drawn from two sources with evaluative terminology.

Against Option 2:

In Source 1, Lewis Elliot supports the Trident nuclear programme and the retention of Faslane.

However, a majority of the public in Inverbank do not want it renewed and want the base closed (Source 3).

2 marks – evaluative terminology with limited evidence.

Credit reference to aspects of the following:

▶ The party supports fairer gender representation in parliament and wants more women MPs – so Lewis Elliot should not be chosen.

▶ Again in Source 3, the opinion poll shows a clear majority for having more women MPs.

25 You must decide which option to recommend, either Hilary Kennedy (Option 1) or Ben Curtis (Option 2).

    (i)   Using Sources 1, 2 and 3, which option would you choose?

    (ii) Give reasons to support your choice.

    (iii) Explain why you did not choose the other option.

    Your answer must be based on all **three** sources.

    You can be credited in a number of ways **up to a maximum of 10 marks.**

Possible approaches to answering the question:

For Option 1:

One reason why I have chosen Option 1 is because Hilary believes that the economy is an important issue for voters.

1 mark – evidence drawn from Source 1.

One reason why I have chosen Option 1 is because Source 1 shows that the economy is an important issue for voters. This is backed up by evidence from Source 2 which says that she will grow the economy if she is elected. This means that she will meet the needs of the voters.

3 marks – detailed evidence drawn from two sources with evaluative terminology.

Hilary is the best option because she believes that the economy is the most important issue for Pimlico. This is from Source 2. This is backed up by evidence from Source 3 which shows that 86% of voters believe the economy to be the most important issue.

2 marks – evidence drawn from Sources 2 and 3.

Against Option 1:

She said that voters are worried about terrorism but the sources show that only 31% of voters agree that terrorism is an issue.

2 marks – evaluative terminology with limited evidence.

Reference to aspects of the following will be credited:

▶ Healthcare as an important issue for voters.

▶ Jobs and the economy are important.

For Option 2:

Option 2 would be the best choice as Ben Curtis said in Source 2 that he would focus on tourism in order to grow the economy and create jobs. Source 3 shows that tourism is an important issue for voters.

2 marks – evidence drawn from Sources 2 and 3.

Option 2 would be the best choice as Ben Curtis said in Source 2 that he would focus on tourism in order to grow the economy and create jobs. Source 3 shows that tourism is an important issue for voters. This means that Option 2 is the best candidate to meet and match the needs of the voters.

3 marks – detailed evidence drawn from two sources with evaluative terminology.

Against Option 2:

He would be tough on immigration. However, voters don't rate this issue highly.

2 marks – evaluative terminology with limited evidence.

Reference to aspects of the following will be credited:

▶ Economic issues are important to voters.

▶ Law and order priorities and issues.

Test your evaluation of sources: to support and oppose a viewpoint

26 Using Sources 1, 2 and 3, give reasons to support and oppose the view of Ryan Willis.

In your answer you must:

▶ give evidence from the sources that support Ryan Willis' view and

▶ give evidence from the sources that oppose Ryan Willis' view.

Your answer must be based on all **three** sources.

You can be credited in a number of ways **up to a maximum of 10 marks.**

Possible approaches to answering the question:

Evidence to support the view of Ryan Wills:

Sam Gunn feels that he is being exploited by his employer.

1 mark – accurate use of Source 1 but minimal development.

Sam Gunn feels that he is being exploited by his employer as in one week he might only work eight hours but is not allowed to take another job.

2 marks – accurate use of information from different parts of Source 1.

Sam Gunn feels that he is being exploited by his employer as he is not guaranteed set weekly hours so sometimes he has to use food banks as he does not have enough money. Source 2 says that 50% of those on zero-hours contracts want more working hours compared to only 10% of workers on set contracts.

3 marks – accurate use of information from Sources 1 and 2 with evaluative comment.

Reference to aspects of the following will also be credited:

▶ Employers avoid redundancy payments and pension contributions (Source 1).

▶ In some months workers have to take out payday loans with high interest (Source 1).

▶ Gross weekly pay for zero-hours contracts is about half of that for non zero-hours contracts and the hours worked are 21 hours compared to 33 hours (Source 3).

Evidence to oppose the view of Ryan Wills:

Ryan is wrong as many workers are happy to have zero-hours contracts as it gives flexibility. Retired Michelle Kelly enjoys her contract as it brings in extra money and she still has time to see her grandchildren. So she does not feel exploited.

2 marks – accurate use of Source 1 with evaluative comment.

These contracts enable many workers to control their work–life balance – for example, it suits students who can combine their studies with earning money. This is supported in the survey of employment satisfaction where more people on zero-hours contracts feel they have the correct work–life balance (65% compared to 58%).

2 marks – accurate use of information from Sources 1 and 2.

Ryan is wrong as many workers are happy to have zero-hours contracts as it gives flexibility to retired workers and students – two examples of those who do not feel exploited. The elderly can enjoy earning more money by working part-time but still have time to enjoy their retirement. In the survey on employment satisfaction the figure for zero-hours contracts is higher for work–life balance.

3 marks – accurate use of information from Sources 1 and 2 with evaluative comment.

Reference to aspects of the following will also be credited:

▶ For those who are retired this contract keeps them active (Source 1).

▶ In many cases both the employer and employee are happy with this contract (Source 1).

▶ 50% of those on a zero-hours contract do not want more hours (Source 2).

27 Using Sources 1, 2 and 3, give reasons to support and oppose the views of Bruce Hart.

In your answer you must:

▶ give evidence from the sources that support Bruce Hart's view and

▶ give evidence from the sources that oppose Bruce Hart's view.

Your answer must be based on all **three** sources.

You can be credited in a number of ways **up to a maximum of 10 marks**.

Possible approaches to answering the question:

Evidence to support the view of Bruce Hart:

One reason to support the view of Bruce Hart is that Source 1 states the 'No' campaign won the referendum.

1 mark – accurate use of Source 1 but minimal development.

One reason to support the view of Bruce Hart can be found in Source 1. Source 1 shows that the 'No' campaign won. This is supported by evidence from Source 1 which shows that 'No' won with over 55% of the vote compared to the 'Yes' campaign's 45%.

2 marks – accurate use of information from Source 1.

One reason to support the view of Bruce Hart can be found in Source 1. Source 1 states that the counting of votes was done by council areas. There are 32 council areas in Scotland. Source 2 shows that out of these 32 areas, the 'No' campaign won 28 out of 32 showing that this was a clear victory for 'No' and a major disappointment for 'Yes'.

3 marks – accurate use of information from two sources with evaluative comment.

Reference to aspects of the following will also be credited:

▶ The 'No' campaign won by 55% to 45%.

▶ 28 out of 32 council areas voted for the 'No' campaign compared to just 4 for 'Yes'.

▶ In areas such as Orkney and East Renfrewshire, more than 60% of voters voted 'No'.

▶ Around 60% of voters in Edinburgh and Aberdeen voted 'No'.

Evidence to oppose the view of Bruce Hart:

One reason to oppose the view of Bruce Hart can be found in Source 2. It states that Scotland's biggest city, Glasgow, voted 'Yes' in the referendum. This shows that it can't be all bad for 'Yes' if they managed to convince the majority of voters in a city the size of Glasgow.

2 marks – accurate use of Source 2 with evaluative comment.

One reason to oppose the view of Bruce Hart can be found in Source 2. It states that Scotland's biggest city, Glasgow, voted 'Yes' in the referendum. This is backed up by evidence from Source 3 which shows that almost 54% of Glasgow voters voted 'Yes' in the referendum.

2 marks – accurate use of information from Sources 2 and 3.

One reason to oppose the view of Bruce Hart can be found in Source 2. It states that Scotland's biggest city, Glasgow, voted 'Yes' in the referendum. This is backed up by evidence from Source 3 which shows that almost 54% of Glasgow voters voted 'Yes' in the referendum. This shows that it can't be all bad for 'Yes' if they managed to convince the majority of voters in a city the size of Glasgow.

2 marks – accurate use of information from Sources 1 and 2 with evaluative comment.

Reference to aspects of the following will also be credited:

▶ Over 1.6 million voters voted 'Yes'.

▶ The winning margin for 'No' was not as big as had been predicted earlier.

▶ The 'Yes' campaign engaged with many young new voters.

▶ The majority of voters under 55 years voted 'Yes'.

▶ 'Yes' won in Glasgow and Dundee.

Test you evaluation of sources: 'support for valid conclusion' questions

28 Using sources 1, 2 and 3, what conclusions can be drawn about the 2012 US presidential election?

You should reach a conclusion about **each** of the following:

▶ The Electoral College results of 2016 compared to 2012.

▶ The popular vote results of 2016 compared to 2012.

▶ The link between age and voting behaviour in the 2016 election.

▶ The link between ethnicity and voting behaviour in the 2016 election.

Your conclusions must be supported by evidence from the sources. You should link information within and between the sources in support of your conclusions.

Your answer must be based on all **three** sources.

You can be credited in a number of ways **up to a maximum of 10 marks**.

Possible approaches to answering the question:

The Electoral College results of 2016 compared to 2012:

Conclusion

In both elections the winning candidate had a clear majority of Electoral College votes.

1 mark – valid conclusion.

Evidence

In 2016, Trump won with a clear majority of 74 Electoral College votes, while Obama in 2012 had an even greater majority of 126.

2 marks – with evidence from two sources.

The popular vote results of 2016 compared to 2012:

Conclusion

In both elections the Democrats had a majority of the popular vote, but unlike Obama in 2012, Hillary Clinton did not win in 2016.

1 mark – valid conclusion.

Evidence

In 2012 Obama won with 4 million popular votes more than the Republican candidate and secured a clear victory in the Electoral College. In contrast, in 2016 Clinton won around 3 million votes more than Trump, but failed to win a majority of the Electoral College votes.

2 marks – with evidence from two sources.

The link between ethnicity and voting behaviour in the 2016 election:

Conclusion

Non-Hispanic white people were more likely to vote for the Republican candidate and ethnic minorities more likely to vote for the Democratic candidate.

1 mark – valid conclusion.

Evidence

There is a significant divide among the races, with almost 60% of white people voting for Trump. In contrast, almost 90% of African Americans voted for Hillary Clinton, a staggering difference. The Hispanic vote also favoured Clinton, with only a third of Hispanic people voting Republican.

2 marks – with detailed evidence from one source.

---

29 Using Sources 1, 2 and 3, what conclusions can be drawn about food banks?

You should reach a conclusion about each of the following:

▶ Benefits issues and referrals to food banks.

▶ Benefit sanctions and the use of food banks since 2010.

▶ Food banks and the services provided by them.

▶ The number of people given three-day emergency food parcels.

Your conclusions **must** be supported by evidence from the sources. You should link information within and between the sources in support of your conclusions.

   Your answer must be based on all **three** sources.

   You can be credited in a number of ways **up to a maximum of 10 marks.**

Possible approaches to answering the question:

Benefits issues and referrals to food banks:

Conclusion

Benefits issues are often the cause of many referrals to food banks.

1 mark – valid conclusion.

Evidence

Source 1 states that 'benefits issues such as benefit changes and delays to payments are often the reasons that many individuals are referred to food banks'. This is backed up by evidence from Source 2 that shows that delays and changes account for over 40% of food bank referrals.

2 marks – conclusion with evidence from two sources.

Benefit sanctions and the use of food banks since 2010:

Conclusion

Benefit sanctions have led to many people using food banks.

1 mark – valid conclusion.

Evidence

Source 1 states that benefit sanctions have led to many individuals turning to food banks. This is backed up by evidence from Source 3 which shows that food bank use has increased from 61,488 in 2010 to over 1 million in 2014.

2 marks – conclusion with evidence from two sources.

Food banks and the services provided by them:

Conclusion

Food banks offer users a mix of services to meet their needs.

1 mark – valid conclusion.

Evidence

Source 1 states that food banks offer a mix of services. This is backed up by evidence from Source 2 which shows that they do not only provide food parcels. Many of them also provide hot food.

2 marks – conclusion with evidence from two sources.

The number of people given three-day emergency food parcels:

Conclusion

The numbers have vastly increased since 2010.

1 mark – valid conclusion.

Evidence

In 2010 the figure was a modest 61,000; five years later it was over a million. This staggering figure clearly shows that many people are in crisis.

2 marks – with evidence and analysis.

PRACTICE PAPER 1

Duration: 2 hours and 20 minutes

Total marks: 80

Read the questions carefully.

You must clearly identify the question number you are attempting.

Use **blue** or **black** ink.

Section 1: Democracy in Scotland and the United Kingdom

Part A – Democracy in Scotland

MARKS

In your answers to Questions 1, 2 and 3 you should give recent examples from Scotland.

1   The First Minister has important powers in the Scottish Government.

     Describe, **in detail**, **two** important powers of the First Minister in the Scottish Government.

   4

2   Some people in Scotland choose not to vote in elections.

     Explain, **in detail**, **two** reasons why some people in Scotland choose not to vote in elections.

   6

3   Some political parties' election campaigns are unsuccessful during Scottish Parliamentary elections.

     Explain **in detail**, **two** reasons why some political parties' election campaigns are unsuccessful during Scottish Parliamentary elections.

   6

[NOW GO TO QUESTION 7 STARTING ON PAGE 40.]

Part B – Democracy in the United Kingdom

In your answers to Questions 4, 5 and 6 you should give recent examples from the United Kingdom.

4   The Prime Minister has important powers in the UK Government.

     Describe, **in detail**, **two** important powers of the Prime Minister in the UK Government.

   4

5   Some people in the UK choose not to vote in elections.

     Explain, **in detail**, **two** reasons why some people in the UK choose not to vote in elections.

   6

6   Some political parties' election campaigns are unsuccessful during General Elections.

     Explain **in detail**, **two** reasons why some political parties' election campaigns are unsuccessful during General Elections.

   6

[NOW GO TO QUESTION 7 STARTING ON PAGE 40.]

7 Study Sources 1, 2 and 3 then answer the question which follows.

You have been asked to recommend who should be your party's candidate in the local council elections in Linburn.

Option 1 Candidate Lucas Watt

Option 2 Candidate Sophie Willis

SOURCE 1 Candidate Statements

Lucas Watt: secondary schoolteacher, age 44

I support the housing development as in the long run it will provide new facilities for Linburn and will bring in more council tax. This development will provide lots of jobs for the area and should be supported. The creation of a new industrial estate will provide employment opportunities for all.

With severe cuts to local authorities' budgets continuing to be made, we must try to increase our revenue. Therefore I support an increase in council tax to protect local services. It has remained frozen for many years.

We have a low crime rate and we cannot justify the reopening of the police station. Police Scotland has to make severe cuts to its budget. We should set up Neighbourhood Watch networks to protect our community.

Many parents are concerned about the future education of their children. The influx of young families to the area could lead to the local primary school having too many pupils and having to turn children away. For this reason, I support the immediate building of a second primary school and, within six years, an expansion to our secondary school.

Sophie Willis: health worker, age 46

I am against any increase in the council tax as it will hit hard on those in work and on most of our elderly. Our residents face severe pressure on family budgets and the last thing we need is an increase in the council tax.

Our most urgent priority is health provision rather than education. Many of our elderly residents are concerned that the local health centre will soon not be able to meet their health needs. I therefore support the immediate building of a second health centre. Our schools can easily cope with the increase in demand and so are not a priority.

I support only a limited housing programme so that we can monitor its effects on Linburn. We already have major parking problems and traffic jams at peak times, which create frustration and accidents. I support an improvement in our transport links to manage the increased volume of traffic.

Crime is a major concern in the area and this is reflected in the findings of our Community Council. I will fight for the restoration of our police station. Our elderly population need better protection – they do not feel safe even during the day.

MARKS

SOURCE 2

Linburn is a council area in the West of Scotland with a population of about 6,000. It is an established community with over 80% of its residents owning their own homes. Some are concerned that council tax might be raised; others would accept an increase if it meant no cuts to education and community health budgets. A new massive private housing development is being built in Linburn, which will eventually double the population.

The local secondary school has a very good reputation and standards are high. However, residents are concerned that the present health and educational services will not be able to cope with the increase in population. There are plans to eventually provide a new primary school, community centre and leisure centre. An industrial site is already being built to attract small firms to the area, which will improve the local economy.

Linburn is only five miles from the nearest town, which has one of the highest crime rates in the country. Many Linburn residents are concerned about the growing crime rate, especially the elderly. Frank Clark, Chair of the Community Council, stated, 'More and more residents are contacting me about attempted and actual house break-ins. We need a stronger police presence.'

Profile of Linburn – key statistics (%)

	Linburn	Scotland
Number of pensioners	13	10
Home ownership	82	67
Unemployed and seeking work	5	7
School leavers – 3 or more Highers	40	30
Experiencing long-term poor health	20	18

SOURCE 3

Survey of public opinion in Linburn

	Strongly agree (%)	Agree (%)	Disagree (%)	Strongly disagree (%)
Crime is a growing problem in Linburn	21	28	30	21
Council taxes need to be increased	20	25	35	20
The housing development is good for Linburn	16	38	32	14
The priority for Linburn is a second health centre and a new primary school	20	40	30	10

You must decide which option to recommend, **either** Lucas Watt (Option 1) **or** Sophie Willis (Option 2).   **10**

(i)   Using Sources 1, 2 and 3, **which option would you choose**?

(ii)   Give reasons to **support** your choice.

(iii) Explain why you did not choose the other option.

Your answer must be based on all **three** sources.

[NOW GO TO SECTION 2 STARTING ON PAGE 42.]

Section 2: Social Issues in the United Kingdom

Total marks: 28

Attempt **EITHER** Part C **AND** Question 14 **OR** Part D **AND** Question 14.

Part C – Social Inequality

In your answers to Questions 8, 9 and 10 you should give recent examples from the United Kingdom.

MARKS

8   Living in poverty can have a severe impact on children.

   Describe, **in detail**, **two** ways in which poverty can have a severe impact on children.   **4**

9   The Government provides financial benefits to help people in need.

   Describe **in detail**, **two** financial benefits provided by the Government to help people in need.   **6**

Attempt EITHER Question 10(a) OR 10(b)

10 a)   Health inequalities still exist in the UK.   **8**

      Explain, **in detail**, the reasons why health inequalities still exist in the UK.

      You should give a **maximum** of **three** reasons in your answer.

   OR

   b)   Many people experience social inequality in Scotland and the UK.   **8**

      Explain, **in detail**, why many people experience social inequality in Scotland and the UK.

      You should give a **maximum** of **three** reasons in your answer.

[NOW GO TO QUESTION 14 STARTING ON PAGE 43.]

Part D – Crime and the Law

MARKS

In your answers to Questions 11, 12 and 13 you should give recent examples from the United Kingdom.

11   The Children's Hearing System can help young people in Scotland.   **4**

   Describe, **in detail**, **two** ways that the Children's Hearing System can help young people in Scotland.

12   Police Scotland helps to reduce crime.   **6**

   Describe, **in detail**, **two** ways the police help to reduce crime in Scotland.

Attempt EITHER Question 13(a) OR 13(b)

13   a)   Scottish courts are now more willing to use alternative punishments to prison when sentencing offenders.   **8**

      Explain, **in detail**, why Scottish courts are now more willing to use alternative punishments to prison when sentencing offenders.

      You should give a **maximum** of **three** reasons in your answer.

   OR

   b)   There are many causes of crime in the UK.   **8**

      Explain, **in detail**, the causes of crime in the UK.

      You should give a **maximum** of **three** causes in your answer.

[NOW GO TO QUESTION 14 STARTING ON PAGE 43.]

14 Study Sources 1, 2 and 3 then answer the question which follows.

SOURCE 1

Facts and viewpoints on the use of taser guns

A taser or stun gun uses compressed air to fire two darts that trail electric cables back to the handset. When the dart strikes, a five-second 50,000-volt charge is released that causes the suspect's muscles to contract uncontrollably.

Police officers who are issued with taser guns go on a three-day training course. All these officers are properly trained. Any use of a taser must be recorded and its use justified.

An officer can point a taser gun at an individual which creates a red dot. This usually leads to the individual ending their aggressive behaviour.

A police official stated: 'I know it is controversial, but tasers are an effective and non-lethal way of stopping a criminal in their tracks'. However, innocent people can be tasered.

The youngest person a taser gun was used on in the UK was a 14-year-old boy. In the USA over 300 people have died after being tasered.

In 2014, 10,400 incidents were logged of police having a taser gun, though they were only used in 20 per cent of the incidents. The availability of taser guns may damage the trust that exists between the police and UK citizens.

SOURCE 2

The debate over the use of tasers

Viewpoint of a London Police Officer

I was stabbed with a ten-inch butcher's knife while on duty and required extensive surgery. I was off work for six months and I still have nightmares about what happened. I could easily have died and left my three children without a father. If I had a taser gun, I could have protected myself and the public. I could easily have disarmed the criminal. Violent crime is rising and the life of a police officer is becoming more dangerous.

Viewpoint of a human rights supporter

The increase in the use of taser guns is of major concern. Taser guns are a danger to the public and evidence from the USA supports this claim. Taser guns are widely used in the USA. In recent years several men have died in England after being tasered. Mistakes can also be made by the police, for example, in 2012 a police officer tasered a blind man: the police officer thought that his white cane was a Samurai sword!

SOURCE 3

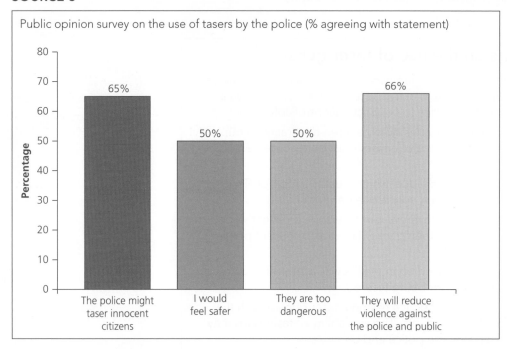

Public opinion survey on the use of tasers by the police (% agreeing with statement)

MARKS

10

Using Sources 1, 2 and 3, give reasons to support and oppose the view of Catherine Daly.

> 'The use of taser guns is a danger to all.'
>
> *View of Catherine Daly*

In your answer you **must**:

▶ give evidence from the sources that support Catherine Daly's view

and

▶ give evidence from the sources that oppose Catherine Daly's view.

Your answer must be based on all **three** sources.

[NOW GO TO SECTION 3 STARTING ON PAGE 45.]

Section 3: International Issues

> **Total marks**: 26
>
> Attempt **EITHER** Part E **AND** Question 21 **OR** Part F **AND** Question 21.
>

Part E – World Powers

In your answers to Questions 15, 16 and 17 you should give recent examples from a world power you have studied.

MARKS

15 All governments have different political institutions.

Describe, **in detail**, **two** political institutions from the world power you have studied.

In your answer you must state the world power you have studied.

4

16 World powers can have a political influence on other countries.

Describe, **in detail**, **two** ways the world power you have studied can have a political influence on other countries.

In your answer you must state the world power you have studied.

6

17 Social and economic inequalities exist in all world powers.

Explain, **in detail**, **two** reasons why social and economic inequalities exist in a world power you have studied.

6

[NOW GO TO QUESTION 21 STARTING ON PAGE 46.]

Part F – World Issues

In your answers to Questions 18, 19 and 20 you should give recent examples from a world issue you have studied.

MARKS

18 International conflict or issues can have serious consequences.

Describe, **in detail**, **two** consequences of an international conflict you have studied.

In your answer you must state the world issue you have studied.

4

19 International issues are caused by many factors.

Describe, **in detail**, **two** causes of an international issue or conflict you have studied.

In your answer you must state the world issue you have studied.

6

20 International organisations work hard to resolve international issues and conflicts.

Select an international organisation you have studied.

Explain, **in detail**, **two** reasons why it has succeeded or failed in resolving an international issue or conflict.

In your answer you must state the world issue you have studied.

6

[NOW GO TO QUESTION 21 STARTING ON PAGE 46.]

21 Study Sources 1, 2 and 3 then answer the question which follows.

SOURCE 1

Progress in development and aid

In September 2015, the United Nations held a special conference to unveil the Sustainable Development Goals (SDGs) that will shape aid and development for the next 15 years. The conference was attended by the largest gathering ever of world leaders and donors such as Bill Gates. The new SDGs replace the previous Millennium Development Goals (MDGs) which have mostly been achieved largely because of progress in China and India.

However, one area that has been disappointing is the failure of the wealthiest countries to honour their promise to increase their spending on development aid. Of the leading nations only the United Kingdom has reached the agreed goal of spending 0.7 per cent of its Gross Domestic Income (GDI). The USA would argue that it spends $33 billion a year on foreign aid, which is the highest for any country (the UK spends £9 billion). However, given the massive wealth of the USA, this is an insignificant amount of its GDP.

One area of progress is in the determination of the international community, with support from wealthy donors such as Bill Gates, to tackle the killer diseases malaria and HIV/AIDS. Africa has the highest number of people infected by these diseases.

In 2016 an estimated 90% of those who died from malaria worldwide lived in Africa. Malaria is responsible for about 450,000 deaths a year. International campaigns have significantly reduced this figure – in 2000 the number of deaths was double the present figure. Swaziland is moving to becoming the first malaria-free country in sub-Saharan Africa (the area that suffers most from the disease).

SOURCE 2

Average wealth per adult in dollars – by region

Africa	5,080
Asia	31,715
Europe	135,977
South America	22,997
North America	340,340

The global HIV/AIDS epidemic by percentage

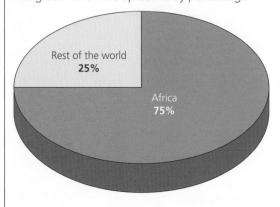

Rest of the world
25%

Africa
75%

Foreign aid as a percentage of GNI (Gross National Income)

United Kingdom	0.70
Germany	0.40
France	0.35
Canada	0.25
Japan	0.19
United States	0.19
Italy	0.16

SOURCE 3

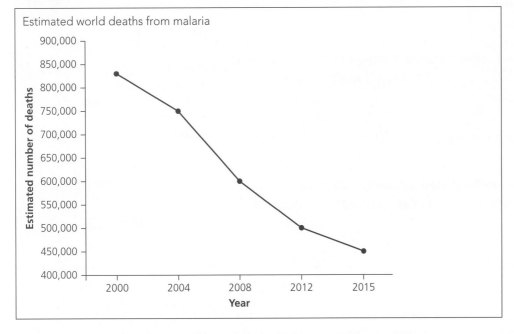

Using Sources 1, 2 and 3, what **conclusions** can be drawn about progress in development and aid?

You should reach a conclusion about each of the following:

▶ The progress made in reducing deaths from malaria.

▶ The progress among rich countries to achieve the agreed GNI target on development spending.

▶ The link between regional poverty and deaths from malaria.

▶ The area of the world most affected by the global HIV/AIDS epidemic.

Your conclusions must be supported by evidence from the sources. You should link information within and between the sources in support of your conclusions.

Your answer must be based on all **three** sources.

10

[END OF PRACTICE PAPER 1]

Duration: 2 hours and 20 minutes

Total marks: 80

Section 1 – Democracy in Scotland and the United Kingdom – 26 marks
Attempt **EITHER** Part A **AND** Question 7 **OR** Part B **AND** Question 7

SECTION 2 – Social Issues in the United Kingdom – 26 marks
Attempt **EITHER** Part C **AND** Question 14 **OR** Part D **AND** Question 14

SECTION 3 – International Issues – 28 marks
Attempt **EITHER** Part E **AND** Question 21 **OR** Part F **AND** Question 21

Read the questions carefully.

You must clearly identify the question number you are attempting.

Use **blue** or **black** ink.

Section 1: Democracy in Scotland and the United Kingdom

Total marks: 26

Attempt **EITHER** Part A **AND** Question 7 **OR** Part B **AND** Question 7

Part A – Democracy in Scotland

MARKS

In your answers to Questions 1, 2 and 3 you should give recent examples from Scotland.

1   Apart from voting, there are many ways that people can participate during elections in Scotland.

    Describe, **in detail**, **two** ways that people can participate during elections in Scotland.

    4

2   Citizens in Scotland should use their vote.

    Explain, **in detail**, **two** reasons why citizens in Scotland should use their vote.

    6

3   Some people believe that the voting system used to elect MSPs has some weaknesses.

    Explain, **in detail**, **two** reasons why some people believe that the voting system used to elect MSPs has some weaknesses.

    6

[NOW GO TO QUESTION 7 STARTING ON PAGE 50.]

Part B – Democracy in the United Kingdom

In your answers to Questions 4, 5 and 6 you should give recent examples from the United Kingdom.

4   Apart from voting, there are many ways that people can participate during elections in the United Kingdom.

    Describe, **in detail**, **two** ways that people can participate during elections in the United Kingdom.

    4

5   Citizens in the United Kingdom should use their vote.

    Explain, **in detail**, **two** reasons why citizens in the United Kingdom should use their vote.

    6

6   Some people believe that the voting system used to elect MPs has some weaknesses.

    Explain, **in detail**, **two** reasons why some people believe that the voting system used to elect MPs has some weaknesses.

    6

[NOW GO TO QUESTION 7 STARTING ON PAGE 50.]

7 Study Sources 1, 2 and 3 then answer the question which follows.

SOURCE 1

Elections overview

There are many ways for Scottish voters to participate in the democratic process. Not only are they able to vote for their MPs and MSPs, they can also vote for who they want to represent them in their local authority and also in the European Parliament. In addition to this, Scottish voters can also take part in single-question referenda such as the Scottish Independence vote in September 2014. Clearly, there are no shortages of democratic opportunities for Scots to participate in the decision-making processes of the nation.

The number of people turning out to vote varies according to the type of election. Some elections are more likely to have a higher turnout than others. However, voter turnout has been steadily decreasing since the 1950s. Recently, in some elections, voter turnout has been less than 40 per cent in some areas. The lack of engagement in the political process by some voters is a worrying trend that could become a major issue.

Across all elections, clear patterns emerge in terms of voter turnout. A person's age, their position in society, their gender as well as their ethnicity and geographical location have an influence, not just on who they vote for but also whether they actually vote or not. The more prosperous you are, the more likely you are to vote. Better-off and wealthier Scottish citizens in social groups ABC1 are more likely to vote than poorer Scots in groups C2DE. Likewise with age: there are clear differences between the turnout of younger and older voters. The votes of older voters are often very influential in deciding the outcome of elections. For many political parties, getting young voters to the polling station is a serious problem. The voting gap between male and female voters has narrowed to the extent that in the 2017 general election slightly more females voted than males.

SOURCE 2

Turnout in Scotland and type of election

Type of election	Turnout
Local council elections 2017	46.9%
General election 2015	71.1%
Scottish Parliamentary election 2016	55.7%
European Parliamentary election 2014	33.5%
Scottish Independence Referendum 2014	85.0%

SOURCE 3

Selected referendum statistics

Election statistics – turnout by selected characteristic, Scottish Independence Referendum

Age	Turnout
16–34	73%
35–54	87%
55 and over	92%
Gender	**Turnout**
Male	83%
Female	86%
Social group	**Turnout**
ABC1	88%
C2DE	79%

Using Sources 1, 2 and 3, what **conclusions** can be drawn about the voter turnout?

You should reach a conclusion about each of the following:

► Age and voter turnout.

► Social group and voter turnout.

► Type of election and voter turnout.

► Gender and voter turnout.

Your conclusions must be supported by evidence from the sources. You should link information within and between the sources in support of your conclusions.

Your answer must be based on all **three** sources.

[NOW GO TO SECTION 2 ON PAGE 52.]

10

Section 2: Social Issues in the United Kingdom

Total marks: 26
Attempt **EITHER** Part C **AND** Question 14 **OR** Part D **AND** Question 14

Part C – Social Inequality

MARKS

In your answers to Questions 8, 9 and 10 you should give recent examples from the United Kingdom.

8 Social inequality exists in the United Kingdom.

   Describe, **in detail**, **two** ways in which social inequality exists in the United Kingdom.

   4

9 There are many consequences of social economic inequality on individuals.

   Describe, **in detail**, **two** consequences of social and economic inequality on individuals.

   6

10 Some people think that attempts to tackle social inequality have been successful.

   Explain, **in detail**, **two** reasons why some people think that attempts to tackle social inequality have been successful.

   6

[NOW GO TO QUESTION 14 STARTING ON PAGE 53.]

Part D – Crime and the Law

In your answers to Questions 11, 12 and 13 you should give recent examples from the United Kingdom.

11 Those in wealthier social groups also commit crimes.

   Describe, **in detail**, **two** types of crime that those in wealthier social groups are more likely to commit.

   4

12 Crime can have many consequences for communities.

   Describe, **in detail**, **two** consequences of crime for communities.

   6

13 Social deprivation can cause crime.

   Explain, **in detail**, **two** reasons why social deprivation can cause crime.

   6

[NOW GO TO QUESTION 14 STARTING ON PAGE 53.]

14 Study Sources 1, 2 and 3 then answer the question which follows.

You have been asked to decide whether the Government should raise the drinking age to 25 in order to tackle alcohol abuse.

Option 1

Change the law so people have to be 25 to buy alcohol.

Option 2

Keep the law as it is. No change.

SOURCE 1

Factfile on alcohol in Scotland

- 84% of Scots thought alcohol causes either a 'great deal' or 'quite a lot' of harm in Scotland.
- Most people disapprove of excessive drinking – only 19% thought that 'getting drunk is a perfectly acceptable thing to do on weekends'.
- 42% of men and 43% of women correctly identified the recommended daily consumption limits for their gender.
- Nearly 1 in 4 men (23%) and around 1 in 6 women (17%) drink at harmful or hazardous levels (defined as drinking more than 14 units per week).
- Studies have shown that those who drink alcohol at an earlier age are more likely to develop alcohol-related issues in later life than those who don't.
- The proportion of 15-year-olds who had recently drunk alcohol fell to 19% in 2013, down from 34% in 2010.
- There were 1,152 alcohol-related deaths in 2014.
- Alcohol-related deaths in Scotland are almost double those in the early 1990s.
- 482 deaths were people aged 45–59, 395 deaths were in the 60–74 age group, 146 deaths were in the 30–44 age group, and there were smaller numbers for other age groups.
- The 45–59 age group has had the largest number of alcohol-related deaths in almost every year since 1979.

SOURCE 2

Opinions on the proposed change in the law

View 1 – 'A great idea. Everyone benefits.'

Alcohol is a major issue in Scotland. Many Scots have issues with the abuse of alcohol and it is a significant factor in the poor health statistics of our nation. Something needs to be done about it. We need to tackle the problem. Drastic problems need drastic solutions. The public think that the Government should do more to tackle our alcohol crisis in Scotland. We need to increase the legal age to buy alcohol to 25.

Currently, young men are the most likely group to have alcohol-related stays in hospital. Not only that, the number of alcohol-related deaths in Scotland is a very big worry. We need to target young people to get them to change their habits and behaviour when it comes to alcohol. Changing the law to 25 years of age would make it harder for young people to get alcohol. This would improve their health and decrease the chance of alcohol-related problems over the course of their life. Young people's bodies are more vulnerable than adults' to the effects of alcohol. The brain continues to develop into the early twenties and introducing this change in the law would lead to greater health benefits for the individual and better health statistics for the nation.

A senior health professional

View 2 – 'A stupid and silly idea. It'll do more harm than good.'

Yes, Scotland does have an historic issue with alcohol. I can't deny that. Too many Scots have paid the price of poor health and a shorter life due to their excess alcohol consumption. Many still do but changing the law and increasing the age to buy alcohol to 25 is not the correct solution. It targets the wrong people. Younger people are making better lifestyle choices about alcohol than previous generations. Many are choosing not to drink alcohol in their teens and this is being carried forward into their early twenties. The ban is unnecessary.

It also targets the wrong groups. Government should focus its attention onto those other groups that are more likely to suffer serious health issues due to alcohol misuse. That would be more effective than punishing all young people by increasing the age.

Many young people do know the risks and act accordingly around alcohol. It is unfair to punish all young people for the wrong lifestyle choices of a relatively few young people who drink to excess.

Current strategies are working. The messages around cutting back and staying within a safe limit are getting through. The majority of Scots do know what their daily consumption rates should be and this shows that previous campaigns and strategies are working. We don't need this unnecessary law change. Improvements are already occurring.

Spokesperson for the Scottish Licensed Trade

SOURCE 3

MARKS

Opinion poll

1 Should the Scottish Government do more to tackle alcohol abuse?

Yes	67%	No	27%	Don't know	6%

2 What measures should the Scottish Government introduce to tackle alcohol abuse?

More health promotional campaigns?

Yes	62%	No	30%	Don't know	8%

Increase age to buy alcohol?

Yes	48%	No	48%	Don't know	4%

Increase tax on alcohol?

Yes	19%	No	75%	Don't know	6%

Limit the number of bar and pub licences?

Yes	15%	No	78%	Don't know	7%

You must decide which option to recommend, either change the law (Option 1) or keep the law as it is (Option 2).

10

(i)   Using Sources 1, 2 and 3, which option would you choose?

(ii) Give reasons to support your choice.

(iii) Explain why you did not choose the other option.

Your answer must be based on all **three** sources.

[NOW GO TO SECTION 3 ON PAGE 55.]

Section 3: International Issues

Total marks: 28
Attempt **EITHER** Part E **AND** Question 21 **OR** Part F **AND** Question 21

Part E – World Powers

MARKS

In your answers to Questions 15, 16 and 17 you should give recent examples from a world power you have studied.

15 World powers have tried to tackle socio-economic issues in their country.

Describe, **in detail**, **two** ways that the world power you have studied has tried to tackle socio-economic issues in their country.

In your answer you must state the world power you have studied.

4

16 Citizens of a world power are guaranteed political rights.

Describe, **in detail**, **two** political rights that are guaranteed to citizens in the world power you have studied.

In your answer you should state the world power you have studied.

6

Attempt EITHER Question 17(a) or 17(b)

17 a) Many world powers can claim to have a global influence.

Explain, **in detail**, why the world power you have studied can claim to have a global influence.

You should give a **maximum** of **three** reasons in your answer.

In your answer you should state the world power you have studied.

8

OR

b) Some groups in society are more likely to participate in politics than others.

Explain, **in detail**, why some groups in society are more likely to participate in politics than others.

You should give a **maximum** of **three** reasons in your answer.

In your answer you should state the world power you have studied.

8

[NOW GO TO QUESTION 21 STARTING ON PAGE 57.]

MARKS

Part F – World Issues

In your answers to Questions 18, 19 and 20 you should give recent examples from a world issue you have studied.

18 An issue or conflict in one country or area can have an impact on the wider international community.

Describe, **in detail**, **two** ways in which an issue or conflict in one country or area can have an impact on the wider international community.

In your answer you should state the world issue or conflict you have studied.

4

19 Families are affected by international issues and conflicts in many ways.

Describe, **in detail**, **two** ways in which families have been affected by international issues and conflicts.

In your answer you should state the world issue or conflict you have studied.

6

Attempt EITHER Question 20(a) OR 20(b)

20 a) International organisations attempt to resolve world issues or conflicts.

Explain, **in detail**, why international organisations attempt to resolve world issues or conflicts.

You should give a **maximum** of **three** reasons in your answer.

In your answer you should state the world issue or conflict you have studied.

8

OR

b) International issues and conflicts have social and economic causes.

Explain, **in detail**, the social and economic causes of an international issue or conflict.

You should give a **maximum** of **three** reasons in your answer.

In your answer you should state the world issue or conflict you have studied.

8

[NOW GO TO QUESTION 21 STARTING ON PAGE 57.]

21 Study Sources 1, 2 and 3 and then answer the question which follows.

SOURCE 1

Factfile

- Organisations such as the United Nations (UN), the European Union (EU), the African Union (AU) and the North Atlantic Treaty Organization (NATO) try to tackle world issues.
- The United Nations works with its agencies in the developing world to tackle issues such as famine or poor mortality and morbidity rates, and promote democracy and better education.
- The European Union was formed to promote economic and social progress within its members. It aims to promote peace and cooperation.
- The African Union works to promote economic development across Africa. It works to reduce HIV/AIDS in sub-Saharan Africa.
- NATO members have been involved in the Middle East in countries such as Iraq, Afghanistan and Syria.
- NATO has been working with its member countries to tackle international terrorism.
- The United Nations' headquarters is in New York and there are five permanent members of the Security Council. These are the USA, Russia, China, France and the United Kingdom.

SOURCE 2

News report

Our correspondent reports that more than 7 million people are now receiving HIV treatment across Africa – with nearly 1 million added in the last year – while new HIV infections and deaths from AIDS continue to fall.

In other news, police in Athens had to use tear gas and water cannon today to disperse rioters who had been gathering next to the Parliament building. This is the third week of protests in the Greek capital as protestors have taken to the streets in protest at the EU-imposed cuts that have hit many millions of Greek workers, pensioners and the unemployed very hard. Unemployment is now 30 per cent.

This is Kate Jones for Network News.

SOURCE 3

Selected statistics

Year	2012	2013	2017
Number of terrorist attacks	6,771	9,964	22,487
Infant mortality per 1,000 (Africa)	78	68	52
Countries with the death penalty	45	41	34
Number of refugees	14m	16.5m	25m
Unemployment in Greece	20%	11%	25%

Using Sources 1, 2 and 3, explain why the view of **Martin Santini is selective in the use of facts**.

MARKS

10

> International organisations are effective at tackling world issues.
>
> *View of Martin Santini*

In your answer you must:

▶ give evidence from the sources that support Martin Santini's view

and

▶ give evidence from the sources that oppose Martin Santini's view.

Your answer must be based on all **three** sources.

[END OF PRACTICE PAPER 2]

Section 1: Democracy in Scotland and the United Kingdom

Part A – Democracy in Scotland

1 You can be credited in a number of ways **up to a maximum of 4 marks**.

Possible approaches to answering the question:

An important power of the First Minister is that he or she is the leader of the largest political party in Scotland and head of the Scottish Government.

1 mark – accurate but undeveloped point.

Nicola Sturgeon is Scotland's First Minister. She has the important power to appoint her MSPs to key posts in her cabinet. John Swinney is Deputy First Minister and is the Cabinet Secretary in charge of finances.

2 marks – accurate point with development.

An important power of Nicola Sturgeon is that she represents Scotland on the world stage and, although it is a reserved power, she can outline the Scottish Government's defence and foreign policy. She is opposed to Trident and the UK bombing of Syria. In December 2015, she attended the Paris Summit on climate change as part of the UK delegation, but also as a member of the Compact of States and Regions.

3 marks – accurate point with development and exemplification.

Credit reference to aspects of the following:

▶ Leader of the Scottish Government.

▶ Directs policy in the Scottish Government.

▶ Spokesperson for the Scottish Government.

▶ Chairs Scottish Cabinet meetings.

▶ Chooses members of the Scottish Cabinet.

▶ Leader of the biggest party in the Scottish Parliament.

▶ Takes part in First Minister's Question Time every week.

▶ Lead role in discussions with other devolved governments and overseas.

▶ Focus of media attention.

---

2 You can be credited in a number of ways **up to a maximum of 6 marks.**

Possible approaches to answering the question:

Some people do not vote because they are not on the electoral register.

1 mark – accurate but undeveloped point.

One reason some people do not vote is that they do not trust politicians because of recent scandals. They also feel it will make no difference to their lives and do not see the point.

2 marks – accurate points but undeveloped.

One reason some people do not vote is that they think politicians are out of touch with the public and are only involved in politics for personal gain. Recently MSPs received a pay rise well above the rate of inflation, yet public sector workers were only given a 1 per cent wage rise. So this unfairness makes the public even more disillusioned.

3 marks – accurate point with development and exemplification.

Credit reference to aspects of the following:

▶ Those who support minority parties are aware that their party will win no seats even with AMS.

▶ Decline in the number of voters who join a political party, so more and more of the public are not interested in mainstream politics.

▶ Increase in the number of the public joining pressure groups and supporting single issue actions.

▶ Not everyone can vote, which includes Scottish prisoners and those under the age of 18.

▶ Voter apathy is increasing.

▶ Opinion polls show trust in politicians is declining.

▶ A significant number of people under the age of 25 do not vote.

3 You can be credited in a number of ways **up to a maximum of 6 marks.**

Possible approaches to answering the question:

Some political parties' election campaigns are unsuccessful because of the unpopularity of their leader.

1 mark – accurate but undeveloped point.

Some political parties' election campaigns are unsuccessful because of their limited use of social media. Greater use would have allowed them to reach a large number of voters and tell them about their policies.

2 marks – accurate point with development.

Some political parties' election campaigns are unsuccessful because of their poor party image or policies. The Scottish Liberals Democrats did very badly in both the 2011 and 2016 Scottish Parliament elections. In 2011, the Liberal Democrats were reduced from 16 MSPs to 5. Scottish voters punished the Scottish Liberal Democrats for their decision to join a coalition government with the Conservatives after the 2010 General Election, and to implement unpopular policies.

4 marks – accurate point with development and exemplification.

Credit reference to aspects of the following:

▶ Party leader.

▶ Party image.

▶ Party membership.

▶ Party funding.

▶ Party policies.

▶ Constituency party activists.

▶ Use of other media , e.g. television, radio.

▶ Support of newspapers.

Part B – Democracy in the United Kingdom

4 You can be credited in a number of ways **up to a maximum of 4 marks**.

Possible approaches to answering the question:

An important power of the Prime Minister is that he or she is the leader of the largest political party in the UK and head of the UK government.

1 mark – accurate but undeveloped point.

Boris Johnson is Britain's Prime Minister. He has the important power to appoint his MPs to key posts in his cabinet. He also has the power to sack cabinet colleagues if they disagree with his policies or are criticised by the public.

2 marks – accurate point with development.

An important power of the Prime Minister is that he or she represents the United Kingdom on the world stage and can outline the UK Government's defence and foreign policy. Boris Johnson supports the renewal of Trident and the UK leaving the EU. The Prime Minister is the leader of the UK delegation in its negotiations with the countries of the EU.

3 marks – accurate point with development and exemplification.

Credit reference to aspects of the following:

▶ Leader of the UK Government.

▶ Directs policy in the UK Government.

▶ Spokesperson for the UK Government.

▶ Chairs UK Cabinet meetings.

▶ Chooses members of the UK Cabinet.

▶ Leader of the biggest party in the UK Parliament.

▶ Takes part in Prime Minister's Question Time every week.

▶ Lead role in discussions with other governments from around the world.

▶ Focus of media attention.

5 You can be credited in a number of ways **up to a maximum of 6 marks**.

Possible approaches to answering the question:

Some people do not vote because they are not on the electoral register.

1 mark – accurate but undeveloped point.

One reason some people do not vote is that they do not trust politicians because of recent scandals such as the expenses scandal. They also feel it will make no difference to their lives and do not see the point.

2 marks – accurate points but undeveloped.

One reason some people do not vote is that they think politicians are out of touch with the public and are only involved in politics for personal gain. Recently MPs received a pay rise well above the rate of inflation, yet public sector workers were given only a 1 per cent pay rise. Consequently this unfairness adds to the public becoming disillusioned.

3 marks – accurate points with development and exemplification.

Credit reference to aspects of the following:

▶ Those who support minority parties are aware that their party will win no seats, even with FPTP.

▶ Decline in number of voters who join a political party, so more and more of the public are not interested in mainstream politics.

▶ Increase in the number of the public joining pressure groups and supporting single issue actions.

▶ Not everyone can vote, which includes UK prisoners and those under the age of 18.

▶ Voter apathy is increasing.

▶ Opinion polls show trust in politicians is declining.

▶ A significant number of people under the age of 25 do not vote.

---

6 You can be credited in a number of ways **up to a maximum of 6 marks**.

Possible approaches to answering the question:

Some political parties' election campaigns are unsuccessful because of the unpopularity of their leader.

1 mark – accurate but undeveloped point.

Some political parties' election campaigns are unsuccessful because of their limited use of social media. Greater use would have allowed them to reach a large number of voters and tell them about their policies.

2 marks – accurate point with development.

Some political parties' election campaigns are unsuccessful because of their poor party image or policies. The Liberal Democrats did very badly in the 2015 General Election, when they were reduced from 57 MPs to 8. The British electorate punished the Liberal Democrats for their decision to join a coalition government with the Conservatives after the 2010 general election, and to implement unpopular policies.

4 marks – accurate points with development and exemplification.

Credit reference to aspects of the following:

▶ Party leader.

▶ Party image.

▶ Party membership.

▶ Party funding.

▶ Party policies.

▶ Constituency party activists.

▶ Use of other media, e.g. television, radio.

▶ Support of newspapers.

---

7 You can be credited in a number of ways **up to a maximum of 10 marks**.

Possible approaches to answering the question:

For Option 1:

I would recommend Lucas Watt as he is a schoolteacher with experience in education.

1 mark – evidence drawn from Source 1 but minimal development.

In Source 1 Lucas Watt, who is a teacher, says that parents are concerned about the future education of their children. He is correct, as the educational services will not be able to cope with the increase in population.

2 marks – evaluative terminology with limited evidence.

In Source 1 Lucas Watt supports the housing development as 'it will provide new facilities for Linburn and provide jobs for the area'. It will also bring in more council taxes. He is correct, as Source 2 indicates that a community centre, leisure centre and primary school will be built, and that an industrial site is being built already. These are all significant developments.

3 marks – detailed evidence drawn from two sources with evaluative terminology.

Credit reference to aspects of the following:

▶ 'Creation of a new industrial estate will provide employment opportunities for all' (Source 1).

▶ Supports an increase in council tax to protect local services and to increase revenue (Source 1).

▶ Supports the immediate building of a second primary school and expansion of secondary school (Source 1).

▶ Massive private housing development will eventually double the population (Source 2).

▶ Local secondary school has a very good reputation with high standards (Source 2).

▶ 40% of school leavers have three or more Highers compared to Scotland – 30% (Source 2).

▶ A majority of 54% believe the housing development is good for Linburn (Source 3).

▶ 60% agree that a new primary school is a priority for Linburn (Source 3).

Against Option 1:

We have a low crime rate and cannot justify the reopening of a police station (Source 1), but Source 3 shows 51% of the Linburn public disagree.

2 marks – evidence linked from Source 1 and Source 3.

Many Linburn residents are concerned about the growing crime rate and the elderly do not feel safe even during the day (Source 1). Frank Clark believes they need a stronger police presence (Source 2).

2 marks – evidence linked from Source 1 and Source 2.

Credit reference to aspects of the following:

▶ Supports an increase in council tax to protect local services (Source 1), however, over 80% of residents own their own homes and are concerned that council taxes might rise (Source 2).

▶ In Source 3 a majority of 55% do not want council taxes to be increased.

For Option 2:

I would choose Sophie Willis as she is against an increase in council tax and Source 3 shows that in the survey of public opinion, the majority of residents are against an increase in the council tax.

2 marks – evidence drawn from Source 1 and Source 3.

In Source 1 Sophie Willis states that 'our most urgent priority is health provision'. She is correct, as in Source 3 a majority (60%) believe that a second health centre is a priority.

2 marks – evidence drawn from Source 1 and Source 3.

In Source 1, Sophie Willis states that crime is a major concern in the area and she will 'fight for the restoration of our police station'. She is correct, as many people, especially the elderly, feel vulnerable. In Source 2 Frank Clark, Chair of the Community Council, indicates that there has been an increase in house break-ins and more and more residents are contacting him with their worries and concerns and demanding a greater police presence.

3 marks – detailed evidence drawn from two sources with evaluative terminology.

Against Option 2:

Our schools can easily cope with the increase in demand (Source 1), but Source 2 shows that the population will double and Source 3 shows 60% of the Linburn public want a new primary school.

2 marks – limited evidence from three sources.

Credit reference to aspects of the following:

▶ In Source 1, Sophie Willis is against any increase to the council tax . However, some accept the need for an increase if it prevents cuts to education and community health (Source 2).

▶ In Source 3, 45% support an increase in council tax to maintain education and health provision (Source 2).

▶ Sophie Willis states in Source 1 that schools can cope and that education is not a priority. However in Source 3, 60% regard education as a priority.

▶ Sophie Willis is against the housing development (Source 1). However, in Source 3, 54% state that housing is good for Linburn.

Section 2: Social Issues in the United Kingdom

Part C – Social Inequality

8 You can be credited in a number of ways **up to a maximum of 4 marks.**

Possible approaches to answering the question:

One impact of living in poverty is that these children may suffer poorer health than other children who do not live in poverty.

1 mark – accurate but undeveloped point.

One impact of living in poverty is that these children may suffer poorer health than other children who do not live in poverty. Their homes may not be properly heated and may be cold and damp.

2 marks – accurate point with development.

Children living in poverty may have a poor diet of cheap foods such as tinned or ready meals. They might not get a balanced diet as fruit and vegetables are expensive to buy and this can affect their health.

3 marks – accurate point with development and exemplification.

Credit reference to aspects of the following:

▶ Ill health.

▶ Lack of material goods.

▶ Low self-esteem.

▶ Poor diet.

▶ Breakdown of family.

▶ Overcrowded/low standard of housing.

---

9 You can be credited in a number of ways **up to a maximum of 6 marks.**

Possible approaches to answering the question:

One financial benefit received by the elderly is the state pension.

1 mark – accurate but undeveloped point.

One financial benefit received by the elderly is the state pension. This has been protected from government cuts made to other welfare benefits such as child benefit.

2 marks – accurate point with development.

One financial benefit received by the elderly is the state pension. This has been protected from government cuts made to other welfare benefits such as child benefit. However, poor pensioners can receive extra money from the government by claiming pension credits. This gives them enough income to pay their fuel bills. However, many fail to claim as they find the process of applying too complicated.

4 marks – accurate point with development and exemplification.

Credit reference to aspects of the following:

▶ Child Benefit.

▶ Housing Benefit.

▶ Jobseeker's Allowance.

▶ Working/Family Tax Credits.

▶ Aspects of Universal Credit.

▶ State pension and other benefits for the elderly.

10(a) You can be credited in a number of ways **up to a maximum of 8 marks.**

Possible approaches to answering the question:

Health inequalities exist because many people still make poor lifestyle choices.

1 mark – accurate but undeveloped point.

Health inequalities exist because many people still make poor lifestyle choices. Choosing to smoke, excessively drinking alcohol and eating a poor diet can lead to serious health problems such as Type 2 diabetes.

2 marks – accurate point with development.

There is a clear link between living in a poor area and having poor health, compared with someone who lives in a more affluent area. Living in poor housing with possible dampness, and lacking money to afford a balanced diet can damage one's health. Again, being unemployed can lead to depression and impact on health. In contrast, someone living in an affluent area is more likely to live in a warm house, to eat a balanced diet and to exercise.

4 marks – accurate points with development and exemplification.

Credit reference to aspects of the following:

▶ Social and economic disadvantages – poor diet and effects of poverty.

▶ Lifestyle factors – effects of smoking, alcohol abuse and obesity.

▶ Geography and environment – poor-quality housing, limited access to local amenities and impact of crime.

▶ Gender – women live longer than men, but are more likely to suffer poor health.

▶ Race – high incidence of heart attacks and strokes. Also more likely to be poor and therefore to suffer poor health.

10(b) You can be credited in a number of ways **up to a maximum of 8 marks.**

Possible approaches to answering the question:

Social inequality continue to exist because some people have low-paid employment that only pays the minimum wage.

1 mark – accurate but undeveloped point.

Social inequality continue to exist because some people have low-paid employment that only pays the minimum wage. Many workers are on zero-hours contracts and they usually earn less than workers on a permanent contract.

2 marks – accurate point with development.

Social inequality continue to exist because some people have low-paid employment that only pays the minimum wage. Many workers are on zero-hours contracts and they usually earn less than workers on permanent contracts. You are not guaranteed a 35-hour week and might only be paid for 15 hours of work, which makes it difficult to make ends meet.

3 marks – accurate point with development and analysis.

Credit reference to aspects of the following:

▶ Unemployment.

▶ Impact of freezing of welfare benefits.

▶ Skills and experience.

▶ Number of dependent children.

▶ Education/training.

▶ Poor health, unable to work due to illness.

▶ Racial discrimination.

▶ Gender discrimination.

▶ Criminal record makes it difficult to find work.

Part D – Crime and the Law

11 You can be credited in a number of ways **up to a maximum of 4 marks.**

Possible approaches to answering the question:

The Children's Hearing System helps young people by involving a range of support agencies.

1 mark – accurate but undeveloped point.

The Children's Hearing System helps young people who are in danger or at risk at home. The parents may have drug or alcohol problems, with the children suffering from neglect.

2 marks – accurate with development.

The Children's Hearing System helps young people by providing a relaxed and protective atmosphere where young people can discuss their offending behaviour. Social workers, teachers and police officers can provide the sympathetic support to enable the young person to change their behaviour.

3 marks – accurate points with development and exemplification.

Credit reference to aspects of the following:

▶ Provides safe and protective environment to discuss issues and problems.

▶ Joint support from various agencies, e.g. social workers, schools, police.

▶ Attempts to deal with root cause of problem.

▶ Provides support regarding welfare concerns and offending behaviour.

▶ Power to remove at-risk children from their homes into secure accommodation.

12 You can be credited in a number of ways **up to a maximum of 6 marks.**

Possible approaches to answering the question:

One way the police do this is by maintaining law and order and keeping our streets safe.

1 mark – accurate but undeveloped point.

One way the police do this is by maintaining law and order and keeping our streets safe. They do this by working on crime prevention. In doing this they will observe the public and patrol on the beat.

2 marks – accurate point with development.

One way the police do this is by maintaining law and order and keeping our streets safe. They do this by working on crime prevention. In doing this they will observe the public and patrol on the beat. The police will also visit schools and give presentations on drugs and knife crime. In schools in Renfrewshire, the police raise awareness by showing young people the impact of being stabbed.

4 marks – accurate points with development and exemplification.

Credit reference to aspects of the following:

▶ Maintain law and order, e.g. police on the beat.

▶ Detect crime, e.g. carry out investigations, interview witnesses, process evidence.

▶ Protection of the public, e.g. security at football matches, initiatives such as knife amnesties.

▶ Crime prevention such as visiting schools, Neighbourhood Watch.

▶ Involvement in court system.

13(a) You can be credited in a number of ways **up to a maximum of 8 marks.**

Possible approaches to answering the question:

Prisons are not effective as too many prisoners reoffend when they come out of prison.

1 mark – accurate but undeveloped point.

Prisons are not effective as too many short-term prisoners reoffend when they come out of prison. With short sentences there is little opportunity for rehabilitation programmes.

2 marks – accurate point with development.

One reason is that Scotland's prisons are severely overcrowded and with budget cuts, savings must be made. A community service punishment or a fine can be far more effective than handing out a short prison sentence. These types of sentences help to solve the issue of overcrowding. This will reduce the stress on prison officers and provide greater opportunities for rehabilitation programmes.

4 marks – accurate points with development and exemplification.

Credit reference to aspects of the following:

▶ Prisons are expensive and overcrowded.

▶ High level of reoffending.

▶ Limited opportunities for rehabilitation.

▶ Non-custodial sentences keeps families together.

▶ Non-custodial sentences can allow offenders to keep their jobs.

▶ Electronic tagging and CPOs less expensive than prisons.

▶ Success of restorative justice especially for young people.

13(b) You can be credited in a number of ways **up to a maximum of 8 marks.**

Possible approaches to answering the question:

The impact of alcohol can cause crimes.

1 mark – accurate but undeveloped point.

The impact of alcohol can cause crimes. A large number of court cases consist of the accused having no memory of carrying out, for example, violent assaults as they were drunk at the time.

2 marks – accurate point with development.

Drug addiction is a major cause of crime as addicts will do anything to pay for their drugs. They will steal to fund their habit even from their parents or other family members. They are a danger to the public as they will mug vulnerable people especially the elderly. They are also most likely to be arrested for crimes such as burglary and shoplifting.

4 marks – accurate points with development and exemplification.

Credit reference to aspects of the following:

- ► Mental illness.
- ► Poverty/deprivation.
- ► Family influence.

- ► Alcohol/drug abuse.
- ► Greed – white collar crime.
- ► Peer pressure.

---

14 You can be credited in a number of ways **up to a maximum of 10 marks.**

Possible approaches to answering the question:

Evidence to support the view of Catherine Daly:

In the USA over 300 people have died after being tasered.

1 mark – accurate use of source of Source 1 but minimal development.

Innocent people and young people can be injured, for example a blind man was tasered after the police officer thought he was carrying a dangerous weapon. Also, a 14-year-old boy was hit by a taser gun.

2 marks – accurate sources of information from Source 1 and Source 2.

Over 10,400 incidents were logged in the UK in 2014, with a 14-year-old boy being tasered. The human rights supporter argues that taser guns are a danger to the public and quotes evidence from the seriously high number of taser deaths in the USA.

3 marks – accurate source of information from Sources 1 and 2 with evaluative comment.

Credit reference to aspects of the following:

- ► The British public have great trust in their police and this trust may be damaged by the continual use of taser guns (Source 1).
- ► Increased use of taser guns is of major concern (Source 2).
- ► Taser guns are a danger to the public (Source2).
- ► Several men have died in England after being tasered (Source 2).
- ► Public opinion survey with over 60% agreeing that police might taser innocent citizens (Source 3).
- ► Public opinion survey with 50% agreeing that they are too dangerous (Source 3).

Evidence to oppose the view of Catherine Daly:

Catherine is wrong, as having a taser gun may defuse a possible threat to the public with the 'individual ending their aggressive behaviour'. In 2014 the police only had to use a taser gun in one out of five incidents. This shows that taser guns deter violent crime and protect the public.

2 marks – accurate use of Source 1 with evaluative comment.

A police officer in London is convinced that the use of taser guns protects not just the public but also the police. This is supported in the survey of the police use of tasers, with two-thirds of the public agreeing that their use will reduce violence against the police and the public.

2 marks – accurate use of information from Source 1 and Source 3.

Catherine is wrong as police use of taser guns is not a danger to all and their use can prevent serious injuries and save lives. The London police officer who almost died from a savage knife attack experienced serious injuries which could have been avoided if he had had the protection of a taser gun. Officers go on a three-day training course and are properly trained. So the police make great efforts to ensure that the danger to the public is kept to a minimum.

3 marks – accurate source of information from Sources 1 and 2 with evaluative comment.

Credit reference to aspects of the following:

- ► Any use of a taser gun must be recorded by the police and justified (Source 1).
- ► Tasers are an effective and non-lethal way of stopping a possible violent incident (Source 1).
- ► Violent crime is increasing and the job of a police officer is becoming more dangerous (Source 2).
- ► The police officer states: 'If I had a taser gun, I could have protected myself and the public.' (Source 2).
- ► A significant number of those surveyed would feel safer if the police had taser guns (Source 3).

Section 3: International Issues

Part E – World Powers

15 You can be credited in a number of ways **up to a maximum of 4 marks.**

Possible approaches to answering the question:

USA:

The American Constitution outlines the powers of the different institutions, such as the President and Congress.

1 mark – accurate but undeveloped point.

The American Constitution outlines the powers of the different institutions, such as the President and Congress. The President is elected every four years and they are in charge of the executive with wide powers to hire and sack their cabinet.

2 marks – accurate point with development.

The American Constitution outlines the powers of the different institutions. such as the President and Congress. The President is elected every four years and they are in charge of the executive with wide powers to hire and sack their cabinet. The President can propose laws which can be implemented or rejected by Congress and judged legal by the Supreme Court.

3 marks – accurate coverage of more than one institution with development.

Credit reference to aspects of the following:

▶ Different levels of government.

▶ Democractic structure.

▶ Voting in elections at various levels.

▶ Separation powers.

▶ Role of judiciary.

China:

One right Chinese citizens have is to elect their representatives at the local level, such as elections to Village Committees.

1 mark – accurate but undeveloped point.

One right Chinese citizens have is to be able to protest against local political decisions. However, they need permission from the Communist party who need to approve the protests.

2 marks – accurate with development.

The Chinese Constitution grants the Chinese people many political rights but they are linked to the responsibilities of being loyal to the Communist party and its ideology. If you criticise the government or try to set up a new political party you will be arrested.

3 marks – accurate point with development, exemplification and analysis.

Credit reference to aspects of the following:

▶ The right to vote in local elections.

▶ The right to join the Communist party.

▶ The right to freedom of speech in public and online to strengthen Communism.

▶ The right to protest, but only if permission is given.

---

16 You can be credited in a number of ways up to **a maximum of 6 marks**.

Possible approaches to answering the question:

USA:

The USA is a member of numerous international organisations such as the UN.

1 mark – accurate but undeveloped point.

The USA is a member of numerous international organisations such as the UN. It is a permanent member of the Security Council which makes the big decisions.

2 marks – accurate point with development.

The USA is a member of numerous international organisations such as the UN. It is a permanent member of the Security Council which makes the big decisions. The USA provides around 30% of the peacekeeping budget.

3 marks – accurate point with development and exemplification.

Credit references to aspects of the following:

▶ Permanent member of the security council of the UN with powers to use the veto.

▶ Membership of G7 and G20 group of countries.

▶ Leader and biggest contributor to NATO.

▶ Examples of political influence on the global stage.

China:

China is a member of numerous international organisations such as the UN.

1 mark – accurate but undeveloped point.

China is a member of numerous international organisations such as the UN. It is a permanent member of the Security Council which makes the big decisions.

2 marks – accurate point with development.

China is a member of numerous international organisations such as the UN. It is a permanent member of the Security Council which makes the big decisions. China donates the second-largest amount to the UN budget.

3 marks – accurate point with development and exemplification.

Credit reference to aspects of the following:

▶ Permanent member of the security council of the UN with powers to use a veto.

▶ Membership of G20 group of countries.

▶ Growing political influence around the world through its investments in other countries.

▶ Examples of political influence on the global stage.

---

17 You can be credited in a number of ways **up to a maximum of 6 marks**.

Possible approaches to answering the question:

USA:

In the USA health inequalities still exist despite the introduction of the Affordable Care Act.

1 mark – accurate but undeveloped point.

Unlike the UK, the USA does not have a state-funded national health service. Health provision is provided mostly through private health insurance companies. Many people cannot afford the payments and cannot always get the treatment they need.

2 marks – accurate with development.

In the USA health inequalities continue to exist. One reason is that you have to buy private medical insurance. This means that many poor people have only limited or no health insurance despite help from Obama's reforms. This means that they receive only very basic medical care. This can shorten their lives or prevent them from working. This can impact most on ethnic minorities, with one in four Hispanic people having no health insurance compared to one in ten white people.

4 marks – accurate point with development, exemplification and analysis.

China:

In China there are inequalities between rural and urban areas.

1 mark – accurate but undeveloped point.

In China there are inequalities between the poor rural communities and the rich urban areas. In the rural areas most people work in low-paid agricultural jobs and have a low standard of living. In contrast many urban workers have highly paid employment working for the state or multinational companies.

2 marks – accurate with development.

In China there are vast inequalities in terms of housing, education and income between the migrant workers who come to the cities for work and those with a residence permit and middle-class background. Migrant workers receive low pay and have to live in substandard homes. If they bring their families they will find it difficult to get them into schools. Middle-class Chinese have high incomes and live in modern homes. Migrant workers are caught in the poverty trap.

3 marks – accurate point with development, exemplification and analysis.

For all countries chosen, credit reference to aspects of the following:

▶ Educational inequalities.

▶ Issues relating to health and healthcare inequalities.

▶ Income and employment inequalities.

▶ Housing inequalities.

Part F – World Issues

18 You can be credited in a number of ways up to **a maximum of 4 marks.**

Possible approaches to answering the question

Issue: Lack of development in Africa

The consequence of poverty in an African country is that many people experience hunger.

1 mark – accurate but undeveloped point.

The consequence of poverty in an African country is that many people experience hunger. At present a civil war is taking place in South Sudan causing food shortages, and over a million people face the threat of famine.

2 marks – accurate with development.

The consequence of poverty in an African country is that many people experience hunger. At present a civil war is taking place in South Sudan causing food shortages. A consequence of this is that over a million people face the threat of famine which will lead to mass starvation and death.

4 marks – accurate with development and exemplification.

Credit reference to aspects of the following:

▶ Poverty.

▶ Hunger (famine).

▶ Disease.

▶ Migration refugees.

▶ Terrorism.

▶ Child soldiers.

19 You can be credited in a number of ways up to **a maximum of 6 marks.**

Possible approaches to answering the question: Lack of development in Africa

One cause of the lack of development in Africa is corrupt governments.

1 mark – accurate but undeveloped point.

One cause of the lack of development in Africa is corrupt governments. It is estimated that government corruption costs $60 billion in Africa every year.

2 marks – accurate with development.

One cause of the lack of development in Africa is conflict/civil war between different ethnic groups. After a long civil war Sudan divided into two countries. Unfortunately the government in the new country of South Sudan failed to maintain peace and prosperity. The two main tribes that formed the coalition government began fighting and so ethnic rivalry and tension led to civil war.

4 marks – accurate point with development, exemplification and analysis.

Credit reference to aspects of the following:

▶ Nationalism – Palestine/Israel.

▶ Neighbouring tension – Ukraine/Russia.

▶ Under-development in Africa – poverty/poor health/poor education.

▶ Terrorism and religious extremism – Al Qaeda, ISIS.

20 You can be credited in a number of ways **up to a maximum of 6 marks.**

Possible approaches to answering the question:

NATO and the EU have used both diplomacy and sanctions against Russia to persuade it not to support rebels in Ukraine but with no success.

1 mark – accurate but undeveloped point.

The UN has failed to end the ongoing conflict between Israel and Palestine. The Israeli Government has ignored the UN resolution to build no more settlements and Hamas continues to attack Israeli citizens.

2 marks – accurate with development.

UN action to support the new country of South Sudan has failed to ensure a peaceful and prosperous future. Despite providing economic aid to the new government to ensure political stability, a civil war broke out. This has been a disaster for its citizens. Since December 2013 more than a million people have fled the country to become refugees in neighbouring states, schools have closed and massive food shortages now exist. The UN has organised peace talks and hopes that the ceasefire will last.

4 marks – accurate point with development, exemplification and analysis.

Credit reference to aspects of the following:

▶ Child soldiers – War Child has had success in the DRC in rehabilitating and reintegrating children involved in conflict back into normal life.

▶ Failure – much of the DRC is still in conflict and turmoil.

▶ Syria – the UN has been successful in feeding and housing refugees in neighbouring countries.

▶ Syria – the failure of the UN to agree collective action – Russian veto.

▶ Libya – success with NATO military power deposing a dictatorship.

▶ Libya – failure as tribal/religious conflict makes progress difficult.

---

21 You can be credited in a number of ways **up to a maximum of 10 marks.**

Possible approaches to answering the question:

The progress made in reducing deaths from malaria.

Conclusion

Significant progress has been made in reducing deaths from malaria.

1 mark – valid conclusion.

Evidence

The number of deaths since 2000 has been almost halved. In 2000 over 0.8 million people died from malaria; in 2015 it was 450,000. Swaziland could soon become the first country in sub-Saharan Africa to eradicate the disease.

2 marks – information from two sources.

The progress among rich countries to achieve the agreed GNI target on development spending.

Conclusion

Progress has been very poor, with only one country achieving the agreed target.

1 mark – valid conclusion.

Evidence

Only the UK's contribution of 0.7% of GNI has reached the target, with the USA only contributing 0.19% of its GNI. Italy has contributed even less than the USA with a miserly figure of 0.16%.

2 marks – information from one source.

The link between regional poverty and deaths from malaria.

Conclusion

The poorest region in the world has the highest number of deaths from malaria.

1 mark – valid conclusion.

Evidence

Africa has the highest number of people who die from malaria and has by far the lowest regional average wealth per adult. For every 100 world citizens who die from malaria, 90 lived in Africa. The regional average wealth per person in Asia is $31,715 yet it is only about $5,000 in Africa.

2 marks – conclusion with evidence from two sources.

The area of the world most affected by the global HIV/AIDS epidemic.

Conclusion

Africa is the area of the world most affected by the global HIV/AIDS epidemic.

1 mark – valid conclusion.

Evidence

Africa has by far the highest number of those infected by HIV/AIDS. For every four people who have AIDS, three live in Africa, which is a shocking figure.

2 marks – conclusion with evidence from two sources.

Section 1: Democracy in Scotland and the United Kingdom

Part A – Democracy in Scotland

1 You can be credited in a number of ways **up to a maximum of 4 marks**.

Possible approaches to answering the question:

One way that people can participate during elections is by campaigning for a particular party.

1 mark – accurate but undeveloped point.

One way that people can participate during an election is by campaigning for a party such as Scottish Labour or the SNP. Campaigning could mean giving out leaflets in the street about your chosen party's policies.

2 marks – accurate point with development.

One way that people can participate during elections is by canvassing voters. Canvassing means contacting voters and asking them who they intend to vote for. Canvassers try to convince voters why they should vote for their chosen candidate or party, such as the Scottish Greens or Scottish Tories.

3 marks – accurate point with development and exemplification.

Credit reference to aspects of the following:

▶ Join a political party and help campaign for them.

▶ Canvass voters.

▶ Publicise their chosen party by putting up posters.

▶ Help to organise public meetings.

▶ Provide transport to allow elderly voters to get to the polling station.

---

2 You can be credited in a number of ways **up to a maximum of 6 marks**.

Possible approaches to answering the question:

People should use their vote in Scotland as it is our democratic right that many other people around the world don't have.

1 mark – accurate but undeveloped point.

People should use their vote in Scotland as it means that your voice is being heard in the Scottish Parliament. If you don't vote, then you don't have the right to criticise the Scottish Government.

2 marks – accurate point with development.

People should use their vote in Scotland because many people have fought and given up their lives in order for us to have rights and freedoms, such as the right to vote, and if we don't vote then we are disrespecting the sacrifice that many Scottish people have made fighting for our right to vote.

3 marks – accurate point with development and exemplification.

Credit reference to aspects of the following:

▶ Voting is a democratic right in Scotland. Many countries around the world don't have the same rights as us. We should exercise our rights as often as we can.

▶ If you don't vote, then some people think that you give up the right to criticise the work of the Government.

▶ People pay tax. By voting, you can have a bigger say in how that tax is spent.

▶ By not voting, voters could be allowing extremist parties the opportunity to gain some power.

▶ It is important to vote in order to get a government that represents the majority of the population. If turnout is low, parties are elected with very small percentages of voters voting for them.

---

3 You can be credited in a number of ways up to **a maximum of 6 marks.**

Possible approaches to answering the question:

The Additional Member System can lead to minority government which can be weak government.

1 mark – accurate but undeveloped point.

The Additional Member System can lead to minority government which can be weak government. Between 2007 and 2011, the SNP were the largest party but did not have a majority.

2 marks – accurate point with development.

The Additional Member System can lead to minority government which can be weak government. Between 2007 and 2011, the SNP were the largest party but did not have a majority. This prevented the SNP passing a bill to hold a referendum on Scottish independence. At present, the SNP administration is a minority government and has had to depend on the support of the Greens to get their budget passed. This gives the small Green party too much influence.

4 marks – accurate point with development, exemplification and analysis.

Credit reference to aspects of the following:

▶ Can lead to weak and unstable government.

▶ Can give too much influence to minority parties such as the Greens.

▶ Breaks the link between constituency and representative; we each have eight MSPs who represent us.

▶ Can create tension between constituency and MSPs.

Part B – Democracy in the United Kingdom

4 You can be credited in a number of ways **up to a maximum of 4 marks**.

Possible approaches to answering the question:

One way that people can participate during elections is by campaigning for a particular party.

1 mark – accurate but undeveloped point.

One way that people can participate during a General Election is by campaigning for a party such as Labour or the Conservatives. Campaigning could mean giving out leaflets in the street about your chosen party's policies.

2 marks – accurate point with development.

One way that people can participate during General Elections is by canvassing voters. Canvassing means contacting voters and asking them who they intend to vote for. Canvassers try to convince voters why they should vote for their chosen candidate or party, such as the Greens or Tories.

3 marks – accurate point with development and exemplification.

Credit reference to aspects of the following:

▶ Join a political party and help campaign for them.

▶ Canvass voters.

▶ Publicise their chosen party by putting up posters.

▶ Help to organise public meetings.

▶ Provide transport to allow elderly voters to get to the polling station.

5 You can be credited in a number of ways **up to a maximum of 6 marks**.

Possible approaches to answering the question:

People should use their vote in the UK as it is our democratic right that many other people around the world don't have.

1 mark – accurate but undeveloped point.

People should use their vote in the UK as it means that your voice is being heard in the UK Parliament. If you don't vote, then you don't have the right to criticise the UK Government.

2 marks – accurate point with development.

People should use their vote in the UK because many people have fought and given up their lives in order for us to have rights and freedoms, such as the right to vote, and if we don't vote then we are disrespecting the sacrifice that many British people have made fighting for our right to vote.

3 marks – accurate point with development and exemplification.

Credit reference to aspects of the following:

▶ Voting is a democratic right in the UK. Many countries around the world don't have the same rights as us. We should exercise our rights as often as we can.

▶ If you don't vote, then some people think that you give up the right to criticise the work of the Government.

▶ People pay tax. By voting, you can have a bigger say in how that tax is spent.

▶ By not voting, voters could be allowing extremist parties the opportunity to gain some power.

▶ It is important to vote in order to get a government that represents the majority of the population. If turnout is low, parties are elected with very small percentages of voters voting for them.

---

6 You can be credited in a number of ways **up to a maximum of 6 marks**.

Possible approaches to answering the question:

FPTP can lead to smaller parties being under-represented in Parliament.

1 mark – accurate but undeveloped point.

FPTP can lead to smaller parties being under-represented in Parliament. This is because the percentage of votes a party wins does not represent the percentage of seats they win in an election.

2 marks – accurate point with development.

FPTP can lead to smaller parties being under-represented in Parliament. This is because the percentage of votes a party wins does not represent the percentage of seats they win in an election. In the 2015 General Election, UKIP received over 11 million votes (13% of votes) but only won one seat. This is very unfair and undemocratic.

4 marks – accurate point with development, exemplification and analysis.

Credit reference to aspects of the following:

▶ Strong government is not always good government.

▶ If party support is spread out and not concentrated in a constituency, parties will find it very difficult to get any MPs elected.

▶ There is no prize for coming second.

▶ Tactical voting is possible.

---

7 You can be credited in a number of ways **up to a maximum of 10 marks**.

Age and voter turnout.

Conclusion

A person's age can influence whether they turn out or not.

1 mark – valid conclusion.

Evidence

Source 1 states that there are clear differences between the turnout of young and old voters. This is backed up by evidence from Source 3 which shows that voters over the age of 55 were more likely to vote than those aged between 16 and 34. 92% of older voters voted in the Independence Referendum compared to 73% of younger voters.

2 marks – conclusion with evidence from two sources.

Social group and voter turnout.

Conclusion

A person's social group or class can influence whether they turn out or not.

1 mark – valid conclusion.

Evidence

Source 1 states that the more prosperous or wealthy you are, the more likely you are to vote in elections compared to poorer voters. This is backed up by evidence in Source 3 which shows that wealthier voters in groups ABC1 are more likely to vote than those in poorer social groups C2DE. 88% of better-off voters voted in the Independence Referendum compared to 79% of poorer voters.

2 marks – conclusion with evidence from two sources.

Type of election and voter turnout.

Conclusion

Turnout varies depending on the type of election.

1 mark – valid conclusion.

Evidence

Source 1 states that some elections are more likely to have a higher turnout than others. This is backed up in Source 2 which shows that turnout ranges from 33.5% for a European election compared to 85% for the Independence Referendum.

2 marks – conclusion with evidence from two sources.

Gender and voter turnout.

Conclusion

Turnout of males and females is very similar.

1 mark – valid conclusion.

Evidence

Source 1 highlights that there is very little difference in gender voting, with slightly more women voting in the 2017 General Election. This is also reflected in gender voting in the 2014 Scottish Referendum (Source 3). Although the gap is greater, it is not a significant one with 86% female to 83% men.

3 marks for a valid conclusion with evidence from two sources and synthesis.

Section 2: Social Issues in the United Kingdom

Part C – Social Inequality

8   You can be credited in a number of ways **up to a maximum of 4 marks**.

Possible approaches to answering the question:

Social inequality exists in the UK, as some people are more likely to have better health than others.

1 mark – accurate but undeveloped point.

One way that social inequality exists is when you compare the life expectancy of those in different social classes. Those that are better off – in social groups AB – are more likely to live longer than those in poorer social groups – DE.

2 marks – accurate point with development.

Social inequality exists in the UK. One area where it exists is in the area of education. Pupils from poorer backgrounds are less likely to do well at school than those from better-off backgrounds. This has an effect on university intake. For example, in some Scottish universities, such as St Andrews or Edinburgh, there are low numbers of working-class students, with fewer than 20% of students at these universities coming from poorer backgrounds.

4 marks – accurate point with development and exemplification.

Credit reference to aspects of the following:

▶ Evidence of health inequalities.

▶ Evidence of housing inequality (homelessness etc.).

▶ Evidence of educational inequalities (pass marks, achievement rates).

▶ Evidence of child poverty, pensioner poverty.

▶ Evidence of gender inequality.

▶ Evidence of race/ethnic inequality.

---

9   You can be credited in a number of ways up to **a maximum of 6 marks.**

Possible approaches to answering the question:

One consequence of social inequalities on individuals is that there is a gap in life expectancy.

1 mark – accurate but undeveloped point.

One consequence of social inequalities on individuals is that there is a gap in life expectancy. Individuals who live in poorer areas have a lifespan 12 years shorter than those who live in more prosperous areas.

2 marks – accurate point with development.

One consequence of social inequalities on individuals is that there is a gap in life expectancy. Individuals who live in poorer areas have a lifespan 12 years shorter than those who live in more prosperous areas. Individuals from low-income families are nearly three times more likely to suffer mental health problems than those from more affluent households. These are shocking figures.

4 marks – accurate point with development, exemplification and analysis.

Credit reference to aspects of the following:

▶ Health inequalities.

▶ Lower educational attainment.

▶ Unemployment and low-income employment.

▶ Poor housing and challenging environment.

10 You can be credited in a number of ways **up to a maximum of 6 marks**.

Possible approaches to answering the question:

Some people think that Government policies to tackle a social inequality such as health have been successful as people are now living longer.

1 mark – accurate but undeveloped point.

Government policies have had success in tackling gender inequalities. Since the 1980s, the gap between men and women's wages has narrowed to around 15%. Policies such as the National Minimum Wage have had some success.

2 marks – accurate point with development.

Inequality still exists in the UK. There have been improvements in health statistics with people now living longer than they did before. However, inequalities still exist, as those in higher social groups such as AB are more likely to have less illness and live longer than those who suffer poverty and are in social groups DE.

3 marks – accurate point with development and exemplification.

Credit reference to aspects of the following:

▶ Areas where there have been improvements such as longer life expectancy and better health statistics.

▶ More women breaking through the glass ceiling in areas such as law and business.

▶ The Equality Act has led to a narrowing of the gender pay gap and success also in terms of work of equal value payouts.

Part D – Crime and the Law

11 You can be credited in a number of ways **up to a maximum of 4 marks**.

Possible approaches to answering the question:

One type of crime that wealthier people are more likely to commit is financial crimes such as insider share trading.

1 mark – accurate but undeveloped point.

Wealthier people do commit crime. These types of crime tend to be more financial and business-related such as VAT fraud or tax evasion, where business owners will try to avoid paying the Government what they should.

2 marks – accurate point with development.

Wealthier people are more likely to commit crime that involves fraud or non-payment of taxes. They are also more likely to commit crimes involving high finance and business. The type of crimes they commit are likely to be linked to their economic status and keeping their position in society.

3 marks – accurate point with development and exemplification.

Credit reference to aspects of the following:

▶ Types of fraud – VAT fraud, carousel fraud.

▶ Tax-evasion schemes.

▶ Insider share trading.

▶ Embezzlement.

▶ Insurance fraud.

▶ Use of drugs associated with the wealthy, e.g. cocaine use.

12 You can be credited in a number of ways **up to a maximum of 6 marks**.

Possible approaches to answering the question:

One consequence of crime on communities is that a community may gain a negative reputation of being a high-crime area.

1 mark – accurate but undeveloped point.

One consequence of crime on communities is that a community may gain a negative reputation of being a high-crime area. This may damage community spirit and lead to a rise in vandalism and graffiti.

2 marks – accurate point with development and exemplification.

One consequence of crime on communities is that a community may gain a negative reputation of being a high-crime area. It may damage community spirit and lead to a rise in vandalism and graffiti. People might leave or not wish to move to the area and house prices might fall and house insurance rise.

3 marks – accurate point with development and exemplification.

Credit reference to aspects of the following:

▶ Areas will become run down; vandalism.

▶ Rise in unemployment rate.

▶ Businesses will leave.

▶ Fear created; people may move in order to find safety.

▶ Lower house values.

▶ Lack of successful role models in the area.

---

13 You can be credited in a number of ways **up to a maximum of 6 marks**.

Possible approaches to answering the question:

One reason why social deprivation can cause crime is because some poorer people who are socially deprived may turn to crime in order to feed or provide for their families.

1 mark – accurate but undeveloped point.

One reason why social deprivation can cause crime is that some people who are socially deprived may also be drug users and they might commit crime in order to pay for or feed their drug habit.

2 marks – accurate point with development.

Social deprivation can cause crime. Some people who are socially deprived may turn to crime in order to have the things that better-off people have. They may resort to shoplifting or house breaking to get these things either for themselves or to sell to others in order to get cash for themselves. There is a clear link between growing social deprivation and an increase in crimes such as shoplifting or burglary.

3 marks – accurate point with development and exemplification.

Credit reference to aspects of the following:

▶ Some people who suffer social deprivation may commit crime in order to provide for their families. Growing evidence of subsistence theft, mostly from supermarkets.

▶ Committing crime in order to pay for or feed a substance misuse problem.

▶ Social deprivation can lead to boredom among groups of young people. Peer pressure and boredom can cause increased crime.

▶ Clear correlation between increased social deprivation and specific crimes such as theft and house breaking.

▶ Social deprivation can put pressure on families and can lead to increased incidence of domestic violence and abuse.

---

14 You can be credited in a number of ways **up to a maximum of 10 marks**.

Possible approaches to answering the question:

For Option 1:

One reason why I have chosen Option 1 can be found in Source 1. It states that people who drink alcohol at an earlier age are more likely to develop alcohol-related problems in later life.

1 mark – evidence drawn from Source 1 but minimal development.

One reason why I have chosen Option 1 can be found in Source 1. It states that people who drink alcohol at an earlier age are more likely to develop alcohol-related problems in later life. This is backed up by evidence in Source 2 which states that introducing this change would improve the health of young people and decrease their chance of alcohol-related problems over the course of their life.

2 marks – evaluative terminology with limited evidence.

Alcohol abuse in Scotland is a problem. Source 1 shows that around 20% of Scots drink more than the recommended amount. This is backed up by further evidence from Source 1 which shows a doubling of deaths relating to alcohol since the 1990s. The Scottish people want the Government to do more to tackle this problem (Source 3). This policy would make it harder for young people to buy alcohol and it would improve their health chances (Source 2).

3 marks – detailed evidence drawn from three sources with evaluative terminology.

Credit reference to aspects of the following:

▶ Studies have shown that starting drinking at an earlier age can cause more problems in later life (Sources 1 and 2).

▶ 20% of Scots regularly drink to excess (Source 1).

▶ Doubling of alcohol-related deaths (Source 1).

▶ Scottish people want the Government to do more to tackle alcohol abuse (Source 3).

Against Option 1:

See *For Option 2* below.

For Option 2:

One reason why we should keep things as they are can be found in Source 1. This shows that young people are now drinking less than they used to. Their behaviour is changing. There is no need to change the law.

1 mark – evidence drawn from Source 1.

There is no need to change the law. Young people aren't the problem. Older people are likely to suffer problems. This group accounts for the highest number of deaths due to alcohol. This is backed up by Source 2 which states that it targets the wrong groups and that more action should be taken to tackle alcohol abuse in older people not the young.

2 marks – evidence drawn from Sources 1 and 2.

The public do want more action (Source 3) but they do not want to see this policy. They would rather see more health promotion campaigns. There is also evidence that the current strategies are working. The message is getting through. Many people are aware of the safe limits and many people stick to and respect these limits (Source 2). There is no need for change.

3 marks – detailed evidence from two sources with evaluative terminology.

Credit reference to aspects of the following:

▶ The fall in the number of teenage drinkers (Source 1).

▶ Young drinkers are not the main issue. Older drinkers are (Sources 1 and 2).

▶ The public want the Government to do more (Source 3).

Against Option 2:

See *For Option 1* above.

Section 3: International Issues

Part E – World Powers

15 You can be credited in a number of ways **up to a maximum of 4 marks**.

Possible approaches to answering the question:

The USA:

One way that the USA has tried to tackle socio-economic issues is by introducing policies such as Temporary Assistance for Needy Families (TANF).

1 mark – accurate but undeveloped point.

One way that the USA has tried to tackle socio-economic issues is by introducing policies such as TANF. This provides short-term temporary assistance to families that may have suffered due to unemployment or increased poverty.

2 marks – accurate point with development.

One way that the USA has tried to tackle issues is through policies such as the American Recovery and Reinvestment Act (ARRA). This is sometimes known as Obama's Fiscal Stimulus. The Government pumped money into the US economy and built roads, schools and hospitals following the global economic crash. This led to more jobs being created and more money being spent which helped the economy and lifted some Americans out of poverty.

4 marks – accurate point with development, exemplification and analysis.

Credit reference to aspects of the following:

▶ Temporary Assistance for Needy Families (TANF).

▶ No Child Left Behind (NCLB).

▶ American Recovery and Reinvestment Act (ARRA) – Obama's Fiscal Stimulus.

▶ Changes to medical insurance cover – ObamaCare.

▶ Food Stamps.

▶ Affirmative Action.

South Africa:

One way that South Africa has tried to tackle socio-economic issues is by introducing policies such as Black Economic Empowerment (BEE).

1 mark – accurate but undeveloped point.

One way that South Africa has tried to tackle socio-economic issues is by introducing policies such as Black Economic Empowerment (BEE). This policy tries to ensure that all South Africans have the same opportunities to be prosperous and do well.

2 marks – accurate point with development.

One way that South Africa has tried to tackle socio-economic issues is by introducing policies such as Black Economic Empowerment (BEE). This policy tries to ensure that all South Africans have the same opportunities to be prosperous and do well. BEE attempts to empower black South Africans to own and manage their own businesses. It also encourages them to gain more skills that make them more employable.

3 marks – accurate point with development and exemplification.

Credit reference to aspects of the following:

▶ Black Economic Empowerment.

▶ Accelerated and Shared Growth Initiative.

▶ Expanded Public Works Programme.

▶ National Skills Fund.

▶ Programmes and strategies designed to ensure access to clean drinking water, sanitation and electricity.

▶ Healthcare initiatives designed to tackle the growth of HIV/AIDS.

---

16 You can be credited in a number of ways **up to a maximum of 6 marks.**

Possible approaches to answering the question: China

People in China have the right to vote in local elections.

1 mark – accurate but undeveloped point.

People in China have the right to vote in local elections. This allows citizens to directly elect a local representative and participate in local democracy.

2 marks – accurate point with development.

People in China have the right to vote in local elections. This allows citizens to directly elect a local representative and participate in local democracy. You can vote either for the Communist candidate or for an independent candidate if one is standing.

3 marks – accurate point with development and exemplification.

Credit reference to aspects of the following:

▶ Vote in elections (at various levels).

▶ Stand for elections.

▶ Participate in political parties, trade unions and pressure groups.

▶ Free speech.

▶ Freedom of the press.

▶ Protection by the law.

17(a) You can be credited in a number of ways **up to a maximum of 8 marks**.

Possible approaches to answering the question:

The USA:

The USA can claim to have global influence as it is one of the most powerful countries in the world.

1 mark – accurate but undeveloped point.

The USA can claim to have global influence as it is seen as being one of the leading countries in organisations such as the United Nations or NATO. It is the largest financial contributor to NATO.

2 marks – accurate point with development.

The USA is one of the most powerful countries in the world. It is economically powerful, militarily powerful and has a great deal of political power in organisations such as the UN, NATO, the World Bank and the IMF. Many countries are the USA's allies and it can rely on its influence to get what it wants globally.

4 marks – accurate point with development, exemplification and analysis.

Credit reference to aspects of the following:

▶ Permanent member of the United Nations.

▶ Membership of G7 group of countries.

▶ Biggest contributor to NATO.

▶ Examples of economic, military, political influence on the global stage.

China:

China can claim to have global influence as it is one of the largest and fastest growing economies in the world.

1 mark – accurate but undeveloped point.

China can claim to have global influence as it is one of the largest and fastest growing economies in the world. In terms of GDP, China's economy is the second largest economy in the world and is expected to overtake the USA and become the largest economy by 2020.

2 marks – accurate point with development.

China can claim to have global influence as it is a permanent member of the United Nations Security Council. This means that it is one of only five countries in the United Nations that have the power to veto any proposals brought to the United Nations. It has used its veto to block any sanctions during the Syrian conflict.

3 marks – accurate point with development and exemplification.

Credit reference to aspects of the following:

▶ Membership of the G20 group of countries.

▶ It's a permanent member of UN Security Council with power of veto.

▶ China has great and growing economic power. It produces a quarter of the world's wealth.

▶ It's the second largest economy in world.

▶ It's the largest and most powerful country in East Asia.

▶ China is a nuclear power and possesses one of the largest armies in the world.

17(b) You can be credited in a number of ways **up to a maximum of 8 marks**.

Possible approaches to answering the question:

South Africa:

Many black South Africans who live in informal settlements do not see the point in voting.

1 mark – accurate but undeveloped point.

Many black South Africans who live in informal settlements do not see the point in voting. They live in poverty in homes that lack basic sanitation and electricity.

2 marks – accurate point with development.

Many black South Africans who live in informal settlements do not see the point in voting. They live in poverty in homes that lack basic sanitation and electricity. Youth unemployment is over 40% and they have lost hope. They are totally disillusioned with the promises of corrupt ANC politicians who have become wealthy while they make no progress.

4 marks – accurate point with development, exemplification and analysis.

Credit reference to aspects of the following:

▶ Massive social and economic inequalities have led to disillusionment for many black people and people of colour.

▶ Legal discrimination against black people and the absolute dominance of the ANC makes voting pointless for many black people.

▶ Corruption of former President Zuma and evidence of state capture has discredited the political system.

Part F – World Issues

18 You can be credited in a number of ways **up to a maximum of 4 marks**.

Possible approaches to answering the question:

One way that conflicts and issues can affect the international community is that the international community will often have to contribute financially to tackle these issues.

1 mark – accurate but undeveloped point.

International conflicts and issues often create problems for the international community. Other countries may need to send peacekeepers into areas where conflict exists such as the Middle East.

2 marks – accurate point with development.

The growth of conflict in areas such as Syria has led to increased terrorism across the wider international community. This has meant that countries now need to work together and co-operate in order to tackle this issue. This has had a cost – a human cost due to increased casualties but also an economic cost as countries need to improve their own security and also work with other countries.

4 marks – accurate point with development, exemplification and analysis.

Credit reference to aspects of the following:

▶ Impact of terrorism on the wider community – human cost, economic cost, etc. Cost to the international community of peacekeeping, promoting democracy.

▶ The international community has to fund development projects and development goals. This can be very costly.

▶ HIV/AIDS – cost to international community of long-term retroviral treatment.

▶ Conflict can lead to displacement and refugees. This can impact on the wider international community in terms of care, resettlement and security.

19 You can be credited in a number of ways **up to a maximum of 6 marks**.

Possible approaches to answering the question:

Under-development in Africa:

Many families in Africa do not have access to appropriate levels of healthcare.

1 mark – accurate but undeveloped point.

Many families in Africa do not have access to appropriate levels of healthcare. Children who are not immunised or who are malnourished can die from many illnesses.

2 marks – accurate point with development.

Many families in Africa do not have access to appropriate levels of healthcare. Children who are not immunised or who are malnourished can die from many illnesses. Each day, thousands of children die from diarrhoeal diseases which could have been prevented with access to medicines and medical care.

3 marks – accurate point with development, exemplification and analysis.

Credit reference to aspects of the following:

▶ Unsafe water/poor sanitary conditions.

▶ Low life expectancy/high infant mortality rates.

▶ Gender inequalities.

▶ Refugees.

▶ Piracy.

▶ Child soldiers/death from conflict.

▶ Effects of civil war/terrorism.

20(a) You can be credited in a number of ways **up to a maximum of 8 marks**.

Possible approaches to answering the question:

One reason why international organisations attempt to resolve issues and conflicts is to create a more peaceful and stable world.

1 mark – accurate but undeveloped point.

One reason why international organisations attempt to resolve issues and conflicts is to make parts of the world more stable and democratic, which usually means that there is greater chance of peace and co-operation rather than war and conflict.

2 marks – accurate point with development.

International organisations try to tackle issues and conflicts for a number of reasons. They want people to live longer, to be healthy and prosperous, and to live in a world without war and violence. If they can promote stability and democracy around the world then this benefits individuals, nations and the wider global community.

4 marks – accurate point with development, exemplification and analysis.

Credit reference to aspects of the following:

▶ To promote peace and security.

▶ To reduce the chance of conflict and war.

▶ To promote international co-operation and universal human rights.

▶ To help improve people's health and to increase life expectancy.

▶ To promote increased democracy and stability.

▶ To protect civilians from conflicts and issues.

▶ To promote greater economic co-operation and trade.

20(b) You can be credited in a number of ways **up to a maximum of 8 marks**.

Possible approaches to answering the question:

Piracy is a major problem off the north-east coast of Africa, especially in poverty-stricken Somalia.

1 mark – accurate but undeveloped point.

Piracy is a major problem off the north-east coast of Africa, especially in poverty-stricken Somalia. Some poor people in Somalia resort to hijacking ships and taking hostages.

2 marks – accurate point with development.

Piracy is a major problem off the north-east coast of Africa, especially in poverty-stricken Somalia. Some poor people in Somalia resort to hijacking ships and taking hostages. The fishing waters around their shores have been emptied by factory trawlers and the local fishing industry has been virtually destroyed.

3 marks – accurate point with development and exemplification.

Credit reference to aspects of the following:

▶ International debt – role of Western banks.

▶ Poverty/famine – unfair trade.

▶ Health issues such as HIV/AIDS.

21 You can be credited in a number of ways **up to a maximum of 10 marks**.

Possible approaches to answering the question:

Evidence to support the view of Martin Santini:

One piece of evidence to support Martin Santini is that Source 2 shows that the number of AIDS deaths and HIV infections has fallen.

1 mark – accurate use of Source 2 but minimal development.

Source 1 shows that the African Union works to reduce HIV/AIDS in Africa. Source 2 shows that the number of AIDS deaths and HIV infections has fallen.

2 marks – accurate use of evidence from Sources 1 and 2.

Source 1 shows that the African Union works to reduce HIV/AIDS in Africa. Source 2 shows that the number of AIDS deaths and HIV infections has fallen. This fall indicates that the African Union has been effective in tackling this world issue.

3 marks – accurate use of evidence from Sources 1 and 2 with evaluative comment.

Credit reference to aspects of the following:

▶ Infant mortality has fallen (Source 3) indicating that the UN has been effective in tackling this global issue.

▶ HIV/AIDS rates have fallen indicating the AU's effectiveness at tackling this world issue (Source 1).

Evidence to oppose the view of Martin Santini:

One reason to oppose Martin's view is that there has been an increase in terrorist attacks. In 2012 there were 6,771 terrorist attacks. This has more than tripled in five years, which indicates that organisations haven't been effective.

2 marks – accurate use of Source 3 with evaluative comment.

One reason to oppose Martin's view is that NATO's aim is to combat terrorism (Source 1). Source 3 shows that terrorism has increased.

2 marks – accurate use of evidence from Sources 1 and 3.

One reason to oppose Martin's view is that NATO hasn't been effective in its aim of combatting terrorism. Source 1 shows that it has been working with its member countries. However, Source 3 shows that the number of terrorist attacks has more than tripled. This shows that NATO hasn't been effective and that Martin is wrong.

3 marks – accurate use of evidence from Sources 1 and 3 with evaluative comment.

Credit reference to aspects of the following:

▶ The European Union is to promote economic progress as well as peace (Source 1).

▶ Greece and Athens have seen riots and increased poverty. Many blame the EU (Source 2).

▶ Unemployment in Greece has increased (Source 3).